ADDING VALUE
TO LOCALLY GROWN CROPS IN HAWAI'I

PAR

A Guide for Small Farm Enterprise Innovation

By Craig Elevitch and Ken Love

Adding Value to Locally Grown Crops in Hawai'i: A Guide for Small Farm Enterprise Innovation
By Craig Elevitch and Ken Love

Cover: design and art direction
by Boris Is / www.orangemonkey.co

Recommended citation

Elevitch, C., and K. Love. 2013. Adding Value to Locally Grown Crops in Hawai'i: A Guide for Small Farm Enterprise Innovation. Permanent Agriculture Resources, Holualoa, Hawai'i. www.valueadded.info

Acknowledgments

The authors gratefully acknowledge manuscript review and helpful comments by Steven Chiang, Kent Fleming, Ngaire Gilmour, Eva Lee, Nancy Ginter-Miller, Robert Paull, Nick Reppun, Gerry Ross, Milan Rupert, Ursula Schaefer, and Pedro Tama. Input is greatly appreciated from participants of the six March 2013 workshops held on Hawai'i Island, Kaua'i, Maui, and O'ahu entitled, "Value-Added Innovation for Hawai'i Growers: Making the Family Farm Profitable." The Example Crops section greatly benefitted from substantial contributions of material from Robert Paull, Diane Ragone, Randy Thaman, and Francis Zee. Thank you to all the farmers, chefs, and entrepreneurs who have contributed to the knowledge base of sustainably produced value-added agricultural products in the Pacific.

Sponsors

This publication was produced with funds from the State of Hawai'i Department of Agriculture. Additional funding was provided by the Agribusiness Incubator Program of the University of Hawai'i and the County of Hawai'i Department of Research and Development.

Disclaimer

Contact information

Permanent Agriculture Resources
PO Box 428
Holualoa, Hawaii 96725 USA
par@agroforestry.net
http://www.agroforestry.net

PAR

CONTENTS

INTRODUCTION

Even though hundreds of new crops have been introduced to Hawai'i over the past 200 years, few continue to be economically viable for family farms when sold as generic commodities. This is due to the relatively high cost of labor, land, and necessary supplies to produce a crop in Hawai'i. These costs usually make products from the U.S. mainland and many countries far cheaper than local products, despite the costs of shipping and additional middlemen. The low costs of crop production in many other tropical regions make it difficult for small farm enterprises to compete in Hawai'i. Hawai'i also does not have the same potential for economy of scale in farm operations possible in regions with large land bases.

Most family farms can only be economically sustainable if they sell their products higher in the value chain than generic commodities. This is achieved if family farms harvest, process, package, transport, sell, and provide services in ways that add value to their products. For example, in Kona many farmers who sell coffee cherry (freshly picked coffee beans) to processors cannot meet their costs of production, meaning that they lose money on each sale and the operation is not economically viable (Fleming, 2005). Those who process their

> "The amount of value to be added to a farm product is limited only by imagination."
> —Dr. Kent Fleming, UH CTAHR

coffee, market it as their own family brand, and sell directly to consumers can capture a much higher portion of the value of the finished product and, if properly planned and executed, the time, effort, and resources put into adding value will increase revenue along with profits.

Kona coffee exemplifies strategies for a successful value-added product. Kona's 2008–09 production was approximately 3.3 million pounds (green beans), with a farm value of $21.7 million (USDA NASS, 2010). For comparison, the same quantity of coffee sold in the world commodity market as *generic* arabica coffee in 2008 was valued at about $4.6 million dollars, a small fraction of the amount received by Kona coffee producers. The market value of Kona coffee increases several times when including the value added in processing (e.g., milling, roasting, brewing, etc.) and marketing (e.g., certified organic, estate-grown). Without adding value to coffee through careful harvest and processing, branding, and accessing high-end markets such as the visitor market, Kona coffee would not be a viable commercial crop.

A basic principle of value-added is to differentiate one's products from the mainstream. This differentiation allows growers to sell goods and services

Kona coffee is an excellent example of how a value-added Hawai'i product can compete with cheaper imported commodities.

that consumers are willing to pay more than conventional, mass market products. Using the same business principles as for Kona coffee, value-added approaches are being developed for numerous other crops such as cacao (e.g., Bittenbender and Kling, 2009) and tea (e.g., Sato, et al., 2007). The "12 Trees Project" investigated the market potential of twelve promising uncommon tropical fruits, particularly their culinary appeal to high-end restaurants (Love et al., 2007). This effort resulted in renewed interest in locally grown specialty crops, including a program to introduce new crops to consumers throughout Hawai'i with tastings, chef demos, and informational brochures.

This guide recommends approaches for adding value to any crop for small farm enterprises and will also be of value to retailers, distributors, chefs, service industries, processors, import/exporters, tour operators, and homeowners. The path from idea to market is filled with many considerations about harvest/postharvest and processing techniques, certifications, packaging, branding, labeling, distribution, and marketing. Although every enterprise will have to carry out extensive planning on their own, this guide will help readers efficiently plan their way in adding value to their products.

WHAT IS VALUE-ADDED?

For the purpose of this guide, value-added refers broadly to imparting characteristics or qualities to a product that differentiate it from a generic commodity and enhance its value in the marketplace. Adding value to a product or service leads to higher financial returns with a goal of increased return on investment. For small farm enterprises, adding value involves crop selection, horticultural practices, processing, packaging, certifications, labeling, branding, marketing, and customer service. Selecting which value-added practices to invest in is specific to each operation and should include careful planning. Adding value does not automatically mean increasing profits, so careful planning is necessary to add value while increasing returns on investment of resources. Individual knowledge, experience, and creativity all play a role in adding value to products—there is

Cost of Production

For the purposes of this guide, the terms "cost of production" and "production cost" are defined as all expenses of producing and marketing a product including labor, materials, capital, subcontracted costs, and overhead. Cost of production is essential to know for each product based on realistic estimates or real data because it determines prices that are economically feasible, i.e., prices that cover costs and include reasonable profit margins. *Adding value does not automatically imply increasing profits.* Calculating cost of production for various product scenarios can determine which value-added products are likely to be economically feasible. There are several references for calculating production cost for specific Hawai'i crops based on actual expenses or educated guesses for planning purposes (UH CTAHR, no date).

Value-added methods covered in this guide

Horticulture	Processing
Crop selection	Preservation
Variety selection	Ready-to-eat
Crop management	
Harvest techniques	
Postharvest care	

Marketing	Service
Packaging	Information
Labeling	Guarantee
Branding	Interaction (talking, social networking)
Direct sales	
Certifications	Delivery

no cut-and-dried formula that fits all people, crops, markets and other aspects of a farm business.

Example: Persimmons sold with drying instructions

A tray of five persimmons is wholesaled to a store for $2.50. When a piece of string is added along with an instruction sheet on how to make Japanese-style dried persimmon (*hoshigaki*), the same tray now wholesales for $3.50.

The original wholesale price of $2.50 was 30% over the cost of production. The string, paper, and extra

Craig Elevitch and Ken Love

packaging time cost $0.50, so the $1.00 added to the package is 100% over the added cost, a profitable investment.

How to Make Hoshigaki
(Dried Persimmons)

The written history of dried persimmons or has the Japanese call them hoshigaki, dates back more than 700 years. Enjoyed throughout Northern Asia, hoshigaki brings out the natural fruit sugars and healthy attributes of the fruit. North American Indians also enjoyed a variety of persimmons that dried on the trees.

All you need besides firm persimmons is a piece of string, a knife and a shears or scissors to prune the stem.

Trim the top of the persimmon so that it is easy to tie the string around the top. If the stem is broken off, cut a small grove at the in the top of the fruit so that the string can be attached.

Peel the fruit completely.

Tie the string around each stem of the peeled persimmons. Make sure they do not touch each other. Usually the string is hung under the eaves of houses or sheds where the rain or dew does not effect it. Depending on heat and sun, it can take up to 5 weeks before your ready to enjoy this sweet treat. "Hoshigaki" can be kept in the freezer for up to a year. Perfectly dried fruit will form white sugar crystals around a dark leathery skin.

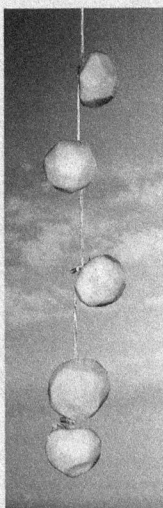

An instruction sheet for making *hoshigaki* (Japanese-style dried persimmons).

Example: Lychee bagging for fruit quality

The cost of production for lychee is considerable, about $2.00/lb, and the market is competitive. Some wholesalers offer growers only $2.50/lb. As a test, young, developing lychee fruit were covered on the tree in special paper bags that allowed the fruit to stay on the tree longer, protected it from fruit flies and birds, and led to more even coloring upon ripening. The bagged fruit were easier to cull (remove excess fruit) with less damage, had a much richer color and had a higher measured sugar content. This high quality fruit was sold to high-end hotels for $4.50/lb. When the returns for this technique were analyzed, growers earned an extra $100 per 1000 lychee fruit (or $1.20/lb assuming 12 fruit/lb) based on $12/hr labor to install the bags (Love 2002).

Lychee fruit bagged on the tree to enhance fruit quality.

Example: Tomatoes of optimal quality

There is a range of tomato qualities in the marketplace, from bland and watery to flavorful and richly textured and colored. An imported, commercially grown, artificially ripened tomato is wholesaled for about $1.40/lb and retailed at $1.99/lb, while a heritage variety, vine-ripened, tomato sells for about $2.99/lb at retail. Due to the perishability of vine-ripened tomatoes, they are often sold directly to the consumer, rather than to a retailer where they might languish on the shelf for too many days, meaning that the farmer often receives full retail.

Vine-ripened local tomatoes command a high price that many customers are willing to pay.

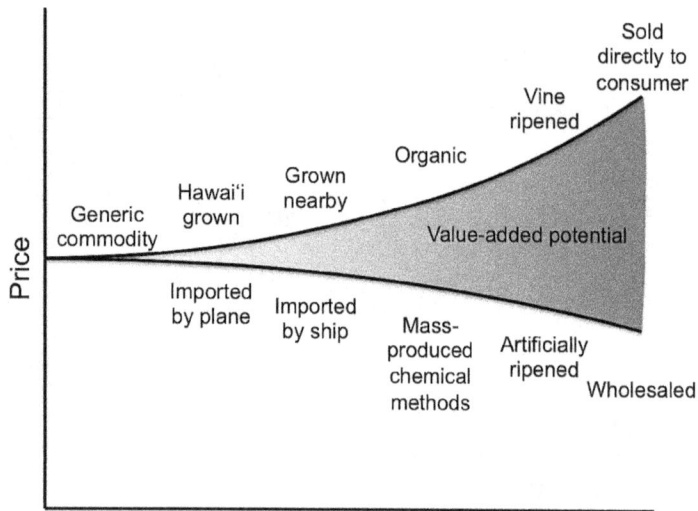

Characteristics of two tomatoes sold in Hawai'i

A comparison of two different tomatoes illustrates how certain qualities and characteristics can lead to increased value in the eyes of customers.

Benefits of value-added

The primary potential benefit of adding value is economic: increasing revenue and profits. This benefit can turn an unprofitable farm enterprise into a profitable one. An associated benefit is the development of unique products that are differentiated from others in the marketplace. This can give a competitive edge as well as open new markets, effectively widening the range of customers for a farm's products. Another advantage is the utilization of produce that was not previously marketable, for example, imperfect or excess produce that cannot be sold in a timely fashion on the fresh market can be made into processed products. Processing can turn these "waste products" into a valuable resource and additional income. Many value-added activities such as processing and direct sales can be done throughout the year, making use of time and resources during times of low production activity. Highly seasonal crops in shelf-stable form can be made available to consumers when the fresh product is not in season. Finally, most successful value-added farm entrepreneurs are passionate about their products and business activities, a benefit that goes well beyond money into career satisfaction.

From the consumer perspective there are many reasons to pay more for value-added products. People are willing to pay more for prepared foods compared with raw ingredients. Many consumers will pay a premium for high quality products, especially if the ingredients are exceptional, such as certified organic and grown by a farmer they know. Local products receive premium prices due to consumers' perception that the ingredients are fresher and more nutritious, and that they are supporting local farmers through their food expenditures. Money spent on local products stays in the community and ultimately benefits the local economy. Consumers who have a deep connection with certain foods, such as hand-pounded poi or hand-made chocolate, are willing to pay extra for the personal attention and expertise put

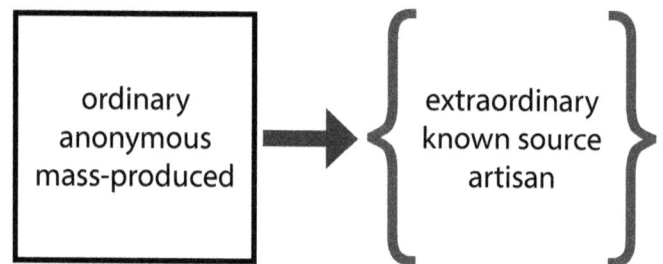

Adding value transforms an ordinary product into an extraordinary one in the eyes of the consumer.

Potential benefits of value-added

Producer	Consumer
Higher revenue, higher profit margins	Processed, prepared, ready-to-consume products
Differentiate products in marketplace	Superior quality and service
Take advantage of the Hawai'i brand alure	Support local producers
Diversify markets/customer base	Support local economy
Increase utilization of harvest	Fresher, more flavorful and nutritious
Greater ability to set prices	Support a cause (e.g., locally grown)
Make use of "off season"	Prestige of "special" products
Outlet for passion in own products	Knowledge about the foods
	A closer relationship with producers and foods

into those products. Knowing the source of food—including a relationship with the producer—creates a personal connection and motivates consumers to pay more in support of those who bring those products to market.

Drawbacks of value-added

Increased costs for adding value can be minimal (e.g., harvesting at the perfect time), moderate (e.g., professionally designed labeling) or high (e.g., costly processing facilities, permitting or certification requirements). Producing and selling a crop as a generic commodity has its own costs of production, while producing value-added products from that crop can add a complex layer of costs and risks. There is often a learning period where formal and informal training take place, as well as a good deal of trial and error. In Hawai'i, difficulties in sourcing materials, high energy and freight costs, and the time to produce a product might cause a product to be priced too high for the market. A higher priced product also comes with an increased level of expectation from the customer about product quality, consistency, and service. Many methods of value-adding require following a new layer of regulations (e.g., health department) and record keeping (e.g., organic certification). Retail sales also require purchasing product liability insurance, adding new costs and hassles that can wear down a farmer/entrepreneur. New and evolving competition is another factor that can greatly impact one's ability to produce, market and sell a product. Overcoming competitors can be costly and one must continually be creative and innovative.

Potential drawbacks of value-added

Producer	Consumer
Higher costs	More expensive
New investments	Less readily available
New skills and knowledge	
Higher customer expectations	
New regulations and record keeping	
New risks	

Kona Coffee is a well established brand with hundreds of individual labels. It is essential to differentiate one's products from the mainstream to generate sales at profitable prices. Examples include distinctive packaging and labeling, certifications, and unique products.

Example—Pricing, competition, and creativity

Kona coffee exemplifies problems associated with competition in value-added markets and the need to differentiate one's products. With an estimated 750 farms and as many as 600 different coffee labels in Kona, there is significant competition. When growers and small processors vie for market share, some reduce their prices below the cost of production in order to get sales. Of course, this is not sustainable and has forced numerous growers to give up the coffee business. Many other growers limp along in hopes something will change. Few sell their coffee based on an accurate cost of production calculation.

The stiff competition in the coffee industry has prevented many growers from being profitable. Too often, coffee growers and marketers try to capture each other's clients rather than finding ways to differentiate their product and find new profitable markets. Instead, they need to go beyond the norm and find alternative strategies for becoming sustainable. These can include certifications, packaging and diversifying their customer base by producing a unique product.

General value-added references

Fleming, K. 2005. Value-Added Strategies: Taking Agricultural Products to the Next Level AB-16. College of Tropical Agriculture and Human Resources (CTAHR), UH Mānoa, Honolulu.

Love, K., R. Bowen, and K. Fleming. 2007. Twelve Fruits with Potential Value-Added and Culinary Uses. College of Tropical Agriculture and Human Resources (CTAHR), UH Mānoa, Honolulu. www.ctahr.hawaii.edu/oc/freepubs/pdf/12fruits.pdf

Peterson, A.R., K.R. Sharma, S.T. Nakamoto, and P. Leung. 1999. Production Costs of Selected Vegetable Crops in Hawaii (Cabbage, Cucumber, Green Onion, and Lettuce). AB-13. Department of Food Science and Human Nutrition, UH Mānoa. www.ctahr.hawaii.edu/hnfas/publications/agribusiness/productionCostsVeg.pdf

UH CTAHR. No date. Publication and Information Central, search for "cost of production." www.ctahr.hawaii.edu/Site/Info.aspx

USDA Sustainable Agriculture Research and Education. No date. Value Added. www.sare.org/Learning-Center/Topics/Value-Added

USDA Economic Research Service. No date. Data Products. www.ers.usda.gov/data-products.aspx

GENERAL PRACTICES

Inspiration, Imagination, Innovation

One's perspective on value-added products might very well indicate one's ability to be successful developing them: it requires an open-minded approach to reaching out to potential new customers, new ways of presenting or processing products, and a good portion of creativity. Understanding the needs of customer groups such as visitors or residents from diverse cultures can lead to interesting ways of processing or marketing products. Often existing customers give comments that spark ideas for novel or adapted products related to existing sales.

The more mundane or generic a product is, the more competition it has (or will have) in the marketplace. The key is to develop approaches to make products stand out from the rest. This is not always easy when, for example, there are dozens or even hundreds of brands to compete with (e.g., guava jelly, Kona coffee). Still, there are an infinite number of possibilities to explore. This also applies to new crops. When everyone has avocados at the same time, what can a farmer do?

Start small to reduce risks—add value with the easiest, least risky, and most inexpensive methods first. For larger investments in value-added, write a business plan and calculate financials for at least two years to evaluate risk/benefit scenarios.

Start small and smart

Developing new products and markets can potentially involve large investments of time, money and other resources. Buildings, processing facilities, land, and marketing materials can cost hundreds of thousands of dollars. Such investments may be necessary to reach a certain operation scale to ensure profitability. However, there are many practices one can adopt at a small scale with no additional expenses that add immediate value to both the product and the enterprise as a whole and can set the stage for future investments. For example, implementing new procedures for optimizing harvest quality can simply be a matter of learning new practices. Harvesting fruit at perfect maturity, for example, makes it possible to sell to higher end markets such as chefs. Setting up an online store can expand markets substantially and allow repeat sales from Hawai'i visitors after they return home. Another example is value added to customer service by delivering consistently high quality product on-time, every time. Customers are willing to reward suppliers with repeat business and preferred status during periods of heavy competition for their business.

Craig Elevitch and Ken Love

Many new value-added products lend themselves well to development in small batches for testing by family, friends, and customers. An extended period of product testing at a small scale can refine the product ingredients, flavors, appearance, shelf life, portion size, and, equally important, help estimate production cost, pricing, and product acceptance by the market.

Market research

Market research identifies customer demand, market scale and locations, and competition for a particular product. It forms the core of a successful business to produce and market value-added products, and it affects crop selection and the range of products offered. This research can help determine pricing, packaging, portions, labeling, ingredients, and much more. For small farm enterprises, the market research process may not be as expensive or complicated as it might seem. Assistance of people who are aligned with the company's visions and goals can be very helpful in starting out, as long as they are able to make informed recommendations. For larger operations, hiring experts for certain parts of the research is often a wise investment.

Knowing what customers want informs the process and helps develop value-added products that will stand out. Oftentimes product suggestions come from friends or established customers. Early proto-

Customer tasting survey of four avocado varieties at a public event conducted by UH CTAHR. Research into consumer preferences can help with variety selection that allows a farmer to become competitive at higher prices.

types should be tested on family, close friends, and business associates to evaluate product quality and presentation. Besides having others do a taste test, their opinions on the prototype packaging and label can also be valuable.

For many consumers, choices are determined by price, so early market research should evaluate demand at prices based on an estimated cost of production. Next, it is important to estimate the size of various markets such as farmers market, high-end retailer, local grocery, gift shop, website and other possible venues. Market size also determines product feasibility. Finally, it is wise to determine the level of existing and potential future competition for a product as a part of market research.

Market research can lead to a successful new product, but does not end there. As customers' preferences change and new products are offered in the marketplace, most successful enterprises continually assess markets in order to improve their products and continually innovate. Therefore, market research is an ongoing process in any viable business.

General practices references

Hollyer, J.R., J.L. Sullivan, and L.J. Cox. 1996. This Hawaii Product Went to Market. UH College of Tropical Agriculture and Human Resources, Honolulu.

Postharvest Technology Research and Information Center. www.postharvest.org

Customers at an Oʻahu supermarket sample chico sapote, a tropical fruit that is still unfamiliar to most people. Offering customers samples is one of the best ways to introduce new products and solicit feedback for development and marketing purposes.

THE HUMAN ELEMENTS

Passion

Small farm enterprises always reflect the enthusiasm and engagement of their owners. Successful operations produce crops and products that inspire their owners, and this manifests itself in many ways including product quality and customer relationships. Passion for the products drives both product quality and consumer satisfaction and contributes tangible and intangible advantages in production and marketing. Conversely, if a farmer no longer finds her/his products to be inspiring, the enterprise will likely whither from lack of attention and enthusiasm. Customers who are looking for special products can sense the enthusiasm of the producers.

Attention to detail

Adding value requires attention to detail at many stages of the process: cultivation, harvest, postharvest, processing, labeling, and marketing. Customers are looking for consistently high quality and supply that justifies the additional cost. Carelessness will not be rewarded with referrals or future purchases.

Tell personal stories

Creating a successful value-added product requires navigating a wide range of challenges. Each farm has its own personality, its own story. People who want value-added products usually want to strengthen their relationship with producers and the food they consume. Telling the producer's story helps customers appreciate what it took to create a product, giving them added good reasons to pay more for it. Successful entrepreneurs communicate their stories in their marketing materials and in person with customers, including a web site with a comprehensive "About Us" page.

Educate customers

Customers are much more willing to pay more for a product if they know about the resources and passion that went into it. Many successful value-added enterprises educate customers about their basic processes (e.g., organic techniques, processing methods) and the historical context of the product so that they can appreciate what went into the consumer-ready product. Educating customers allows small producers to differentiate their products from inexpensive, mass-produced products and those of other local farmers.

Constantly improve and learn

In developing and selling value-added products, sometimes everything falls into place and the "path of least resistance" presents itself. Other times immense challenges arise. The most successful small farm enterprises are constantly learning how to improve their operation and please their customers. They adjust to changing environments and continually adapt to changing market conditions and regulations. As digital technologies become increasingly important, up-to-date computer skills are a necessary part of the process.

CROP SELECTION

One of the most common questions farmers have is, "What should I grow?" There are no easy, straightforward crop recommendations—if there were, many would pick the same crop, compete with each other, and likely create an oversupply and depressed prices in the marketplace. Such an outcome has occurred repeatedly through the decades in Hawai'i; examples

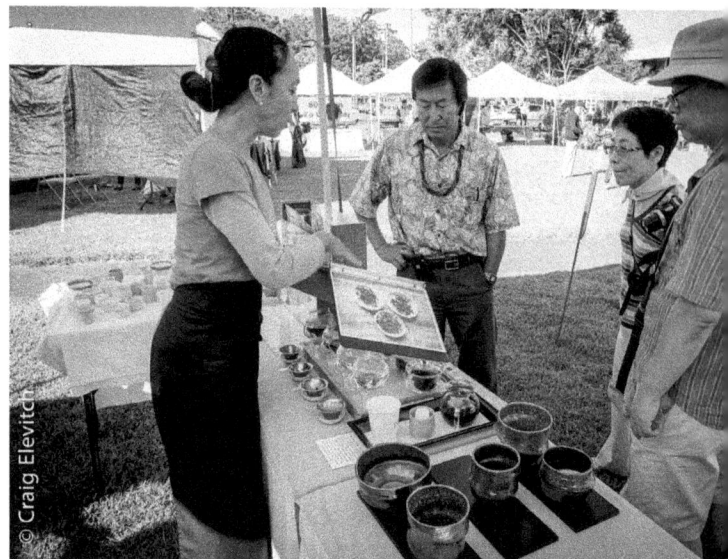

Eva Lee shows customers a photo book documenting the tea processing methods her company has developed over many years. Such consumer education helps potential customers appreciate the value of the products.

Craig Elevitch and Ken Love

Left: Most mangos do not thrive at higher elevations and/or in areas of high rainfall and humidity. In these conditions, the most promising option is to find another crop that would do well. In certain cases, an unusual cultivar of mango that can handle or even flourish in high elevation or high rainfall conditions may be successful. One benefit of the multitude of microclimates in Hawai'i is the opportunity for unexpected competitive advantages for certain crops and varieties. Right: At elevations above 300 m (1000 ft) in Hawai'i and areas with frequent rains during the mango flowering and fruiting season, fruit set and quality will likely be poor. However, such a site might be optimal for flowering and fruiting of a wide range of avocado varieties.

include coffee, macadamia nut, tomato, ginger, and many others.

Choosing what to grow involves a number of analytical approaches to maximizing the value to customers and to your operation. Each crop you grow represents an investment in time, land, materials, and other resources. In the long run, it pays off to take a thoughtful and protracted approach to crop selection, rather than rushing into decisions, where mistakes can be very costly.

Environment

An optimal crop environment will yield the best crop quality and quantity. Put another way, trying to grow a crop in an ill-suited environment puts the grower at an immediate disadvantage in the value-added marketplace. There are several resources available for determining which crops (and varieties) will grow best in a certain environment. Walking around the neighborhood and observing (within public view from roads) what plants are growing well is an easy initial step. Essentially, neighbors have conducted valuable "field trials" by growing a range of plants. With large variation in microclimates and environment (e.g., soils), there is no substitute for actual field-testing of crops in a specific area. Observations over a pe-

What crop should I grow?

Optimal environment
Unfilled markets exist
Timing to crop harvest
Value-added potential
Profit potential
Labor and resource capacity
Personal passion

riod of months or even years are most valuable, as they take account of weather patterns and unusual environmental events, such as storms. Next, an environmental assessment of the site including rainfall, elevation, soil type and analysis, slope, sun and wind exposure, availability of irrigation water and history of use will give a good basis for studying the environmental compatibility of new crops. An assessment of current and potential crop pests and diseases, and control agents available and permitted will also assist in planning. A wealth of resources in print and online cover environmental tolerances of crops that can be compared to the site characteristics. Consulting with crop experts such as University of Hawai'i Cooperative Extension agents, commodity group leaders, experienced farmers, and private crop consultants can point the way to wise crop selections. Finally, there is no substitute for trials of promising crops on a specific farm site to find what will perform best.

Market analysis

Creating a supply of any product should only be undertaken if a promising market exists. However, an innovative value-added product is almost always untested in the marketplace. To ensure success re-

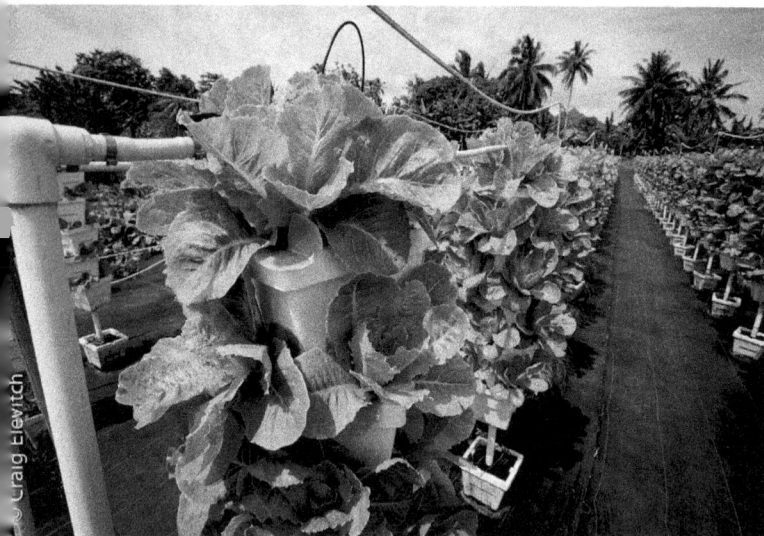

Locally grown specialty lettuces are readily available in Hawai'i for high-end restaurants and consumers who want the best flavor and texture, as well as those who eat organically grown produce. Evaluating the current markets for specialty lettuces is essential before starting a new lettuce operation.

quires a thoughtful market analysis in the planning stage in order to maximize the potential for profitability and reduce risk. A simple start is to ask family, friends, and existing customers which products they are looking for that are not readily available from local sources. Visits to local retailers, farmers markets, and restaurants provide first hand experience of what is and is not available. Having regular conversations with customers frequently leads to a wealth of product requests related to a farm's current product line.

Seek out customers for their suggestions in many venues, including face-to-face conversations, telephone calls, and online social networks. Another direct level of inquiry is to make appointments with prospective buyers to ask what they are looking for. Partnering with a local chef or retailer in developing new value added products can also harness additional market expertise. Delivering samples of potential new products to potential customers can also help determine which crops to develop and what to look for in new ones. Market statistics by the USDA National Agricultural Statistics Service (NASS) reveal the amounts of major crops that are imported into Hawai'i, signaling possible opportunities for locally grown markets. University Cooperative Extension publications, (e.g., Love et al, 2007; Elevitch et al, 2012) also provide insights into market trends and potential new crops.

Understanding competitive opportunities and risks is part of what is termed "competitive intelligence." Since there are no certainties in the marketplace, competitive intelligence predicts trends and helps make informed plans to select crops and value-added products, while minimizing risks such as competitive disadvantages. A grower needs to be aware of what others are growing and selling. A check of local groceries, farmers markets and even calls to local wholesalers also yield valuable information. Being involved with local grower and commodity groups also helps to give an idea of what directions to consider.

Example: Should I grow oranges?

As an example, let's consider oranges. You determine your site is ideal for growing citrus and your family loves navel oranges. You make inquiries with local retailers and estimate that there are 20 other orange growers, many of whom are having trouble selling their crop. Do you forge ahead and try to take the market from other growers, beat the bushes for new markets, or work on value-added products from oranges? Or do you consider unusual orange varieties, hybrid crosses with other citrus such as tangerine (tangor), or grow other unusual citrus types? The

"Look into my rind, tell me what you see…" Forecasting market needs for specific crops requires continually evaluating the market demand and looking for new opportunities to differentiate one's products from competitors'.

USDA NASS 2008 statistics for Hawai'i show that 12.4 million pounds of oranges were imported. Given consumer demand for locally grown produce in general, there is potentially a large unmet need for locally grown oranges. The next step is to determine whether there is a market that will pay a price that covers the cost of production and fair profit. Then, you still have to consider the possibility that there

Craig Elevitch and Ken Love

will be an oversupply of local oranges during the fruiting season. The next logical step is to consider various ways to process and preserve fruit. Marketing fresh orange juice, marmalade, orange Riesling syrup or other value-added products are all possibilities. All of these approaches could work, and the answer may depend on whether you are highly competitive or you are willing to develop new markets for unique products.

Variety selection

Every crop that has been developed by people has numerous variety (or cultivar) selections—the number of varieties can start at just a few, but usually it is in the dozens or hundreds. In Hawai'i, for example, there are about 200 named varieties each of mango and avocado—dozens more are to be found all over

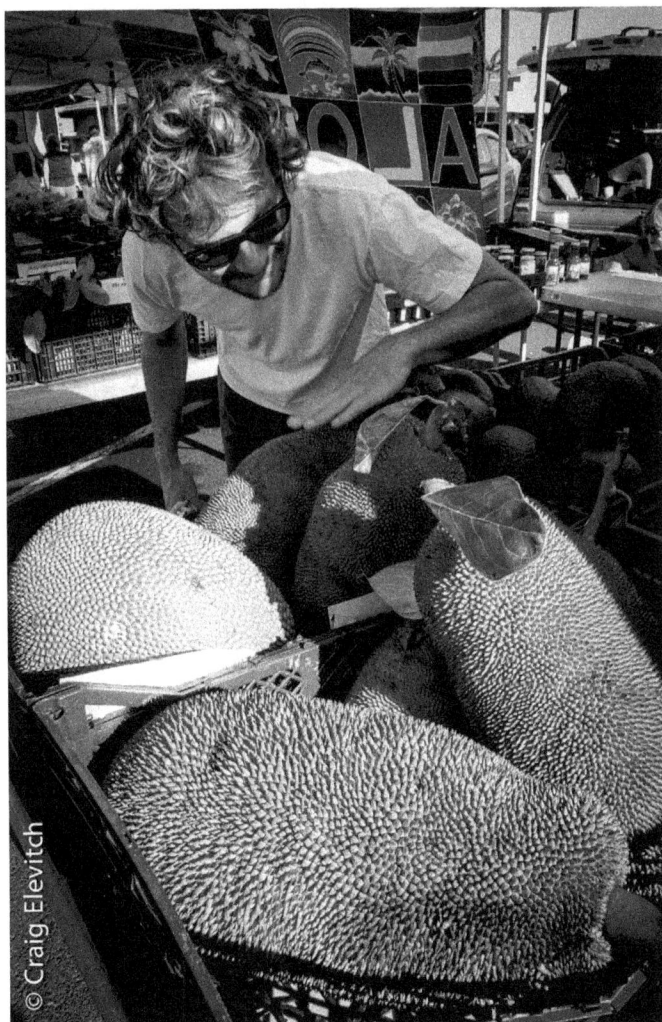

Only so much jackfruit can be consumed or processed at one time, so the seasonal differences between varieties such as 'Black Gold' and 'Zieman Pink' can be advantageous to even out the supply over an extended time period.

the tropics. Every variety has its own unique environmental requirements and quality characteristics. This wide selection allows for myriad possibilities of selecting varieties that stand out from the mainstream. For example, some varieties will perform better and produce more at a specific elevation and rainfall than others. This can lead to a competitive advantage in the marketplace based on appearance and taste. The timing of flowering and fruiting often varies with variety. Late or early season varieties can help make customers happier by giving them a consistent supply, when others have production gaps. In other words, the longer season of availability adds value to a product line. Planting the same variety at different elevations can have a similar effect of extending the harvest. Ethnic or cultural groups often have a preference for a particular variety with a flavor or texture evocative of the cuisine of the culture.

Value-added opportunities in crop selection

Environment	Best quality crops
	Utilize unusual environments for unique crops
Markets	Fill unmet demand
	Large number of possible value-added products
Varieties	Unusual or unique
	Extend harvest season
	Target an ethnic/cultural group preference
Product line	Supply complementary products to customers

Crop portfolio

A diverse range of crops and crop varieties can be a major asset to a value-added farm enterprise. First, diversity is a risk management tool wherein some yields will always be coming in, even if some crops perform poorly. With different varieties and species, there will always be something to harvest and utilize for value-added products. For example, if it is a bad year for oranges due to unfavorable weather, it may be a good year for tangor, ugli fruit, and tangelo, which can be used instead of oranges in certain markets and products. Second, a diversity of crops can be combined synergistically in a product line. For example, ginger, chili pepper, and onion can be combined in numerous value-added products as well as being sold separately or made into their own value-added products (e.g., dried, extracts, etc.). A combination of herbs and spices, combined with a recipe, can introduce a new flavor to a curious palette. A processing facility for one crop may also be used for others, such as a commercial dehydrator, oil press, or still. Generally, those who are successful are using variations on the above and doing it with at least several items at the same time. The best strategy to ensure a supply of crops for production of value-added products is based on a diversity of crops by season, crop, and variety.

Personal preference

There is nothing that adds value more to products than the dedication and personal investment of the producer. This manifests in more awareness of crop health, better management, innovations that improve product quality, and enthusiastic service. Adding value often comes down to the customer experience of the products. A crop that a producer has an affinity for is much more likely to succeed than one that is disliked. Some of the most successful farm entrepreneurs have a passion for their products that borders on obsession.

Crop selection references

Gold, M., and R.S. Thompson. 2011. Alternative Crops & Enterprises for Small Farm Diversification. USDA Alternative Farming Systems Information Center, Beltsville, MD. www.nal.usda.gov/afsic/pubs/altlist.shtml

Kobayashi, K. and H.C. Bittenbender. No date. Farmer's Bookshelf: Information on Tropical Crop Production in Hawaii. Department of Tropical Plant and Soil Sciences, University of Hawai'i, Honolulu. www.ctahr.hawaii.edu/fb/fb.html

Martin, F.W. No date. Selecting the right crop for your location in the tropics or in the subtropics. ECHO, Florida. www.echocommunity.org/resource/resmgr/a_to_z/azch1sel.htm

Purdue University. 2011. NewCROP. www.hort.purdue.edu/newcrop

Anticipating what crops are next

Trends in value-added markets can help with crop selection. It is a great advantage to be ahead of the curve in introducing new crops and varieties, but not too far ahead of the curve, where little or no market yet exists. Current trends include rare tropical fruits for high-end restaurants and hotels, heritage vegetable varieties, gluten free and low glycemic starch crops for the health food market, and herbal beverages and spices for the health conscious. Farmers markets are a great place to watch for new crop trends.

NICHE MARKETS

A niche market is simply a segment of a product market. Usually "niche market" refers to opportunities to sell products that are not available from mainstream suppliers. A niche product fills a niche market. For example, Kona coffee is a niche product, differentiated by its origin and labeling from generic coffee available in supermarkets. Within the Kona coffee market, there are producers who fill even smaller niches, such as roast-to-order and "forest friendly" coffees.

Finding viable niche markets requires research into the products being sold and determining whether demand is being met. The process is more than just thinking outside the proverbial box—it is about leaving behind preconceived notions of what to produce, how to process and preserve, package, and how and where to sell. In addition to exploring what is available and where, developing niche products includes research into what products are *not* available and potential consumer demand for them. Research should include asking existing customers what they are looking for that is not available, and consulting with market groups and experts about individual crops. Research should also determine what customers expect in terms of ingredients, labeling, quality, consistency, portion size, etc. For example, Japanese tourists in Hawai'i look for *omiyage*, which are high quality gifts or souvenirs they will give to friends and family upon their return to Japan. For the *omiyage* market, the product and its packaging and labeling must appeal to the expectations of Japanese customers.

Craig Elevitch and Ken Love

Fresh jaboticaba (left) is still an unfamiliar fruit for most Hawai'i consumers. Preserved jaboticaba fruit, when combined with creative marketing, can be an attractive product for a certain customers, such as this clever product label that appeals to children.

If the crop is fig, for example, and there do not appear to be any opportunities in the fresh and dehydrated fig markets, then it would be prudent to look at niche products: jam, jelly, fruit leather, whole stewed, or some combination of these. Such products may include other ingredients such as raw sugar, wine, other fruits, vinegar, or flour. There are pros and cons to making familiar products such as fig jam, or unfamiliar products such as a savory fig sauce—often the choice comes down to producer preference. To go further into a specialized fig product, the fruit can be cooked down with balsamic vinegar and unrefined raw sugar (jaggery). This savory Italian fig sauce fills a void for Italian food lovers. Selling it in a store that caters to international items or as an item for sale in a local Italian restaurant is also niche marketing.

Finding a successful market niche means appealing to customers who are looking beyond the ordinary or familiar. Language can be used to appeal to a certain group of customers, such as using Italian in the product description for balsamic fig sauce, or using Japanese text on a product targeted to the *omiyage* market. The "Hawai'i" moniker sells, but it is also commonly used to sell products identified with Hawai'i. A fusion of the Hawaiian identity with other regions can further set products apart. Two example products along these lines from the Keauhou Farmers Market include Ka'ū Grown Italian Style Onion Relish and Kona Figs in Italian Balsamic Vinegar.

Example niche crop: Rare tropical fruits

Many tropical fruits have been introduced into mainstream Western markets over the past hundred years, with pineapple, papaya, mango, and banana being accepted and adopted into diets worldwide. For the past 30 years, interest in tropical fruits has grown, with a vibrant niche market developing for "novel" tropical fruits such as dragon fruit, cherimoya, rambutan, pummelo, and many others now available in retail outlets. Today, one could say there is a ready-made niche market for new rare fruits among consumers, chefs, and other businesses that look for fruits that are outside the mainstream (e.g., Love, et al, 2007).

Mangosteen, the "Queen of Fruits" from Southeast Asia, is one of many rare fruits that have a ready niche market.

Niche market resources

Elevitch, C.R. (ed.). 2011. Specialty Crops for Pacific Islands. Permanent Agriculture Resources, Holualoa, Hawai'i. www.agroforestry.net/scps

Love, K., R. Bowen, and K. Fleming. 2007. Twelve Fruits with Potential Value-Added and Culinary Uses. College of Tropical Agriculture and Human Resources (CTAHR), UH Mānoa, Honolulu. www.ctahr.hawaii.edu/oc/freepubs/pdf/12fruits.pdf

Bagging developing fruit, such as young banana bunches, helps minimize damage from sunburn, rodents, and birds, while opening markets for perfect fruit, such as supermarkets.

ENSURING OPTIMAL CROP QUALITY

Exceptional quality differentiates a product in the marketplace and translates into a higher price in many cases. Quality characteristics include appearance, freshness, texture, flavor, aroma, sugar/acid content, nutritional analysis, and much more. Many people do not think of the process of creating quality as starting even before planting, but it certainly does, as suggested in the section above about crop selection. Producing quality continues through every step of crop management, harvest, processing, delivering a finished product, and customer service. There are no short cuts to quality, just good planning, developing good management practices, and constantly adapting and improving—in short, plenty of hard work.

Pre-harvest

From the crop choice forward to harvest day, the foundation of product quality is in the field. Good quality seed stock is essential for the best start—fresh seed from healthy plants gives the best quality offspring. Improved plant health enhances more than just flavor, appearance, size and color characteristics—it tends to increase disease and pest resistance, reducing losses. After selecting crops and varieties, the next step is a planting design that gives plants adequate space to grow both above and below ground. University extension or a crop consultant can help with farm design.

An optimal environment also contributes to plant health. This may include windbreaks and shade provided by trees or structures. Maintaining sufficient but not excess soil moisture is also very important, especially as weather extremes seem to become more common. Mulching and ground covers can help conserve soil moisture and moderate extremes by promoting soil water holding characteristics. Site preparation along the terrain contour can be used to help retain water in the soil, rather than having rainwater run off the surface and cause erosion. In many areas, an irrigation plan may also be necessary. Proper nutrition, measured through observation of plant health supplemented by soil and leaf analysis is necessary to maintain plant health.

Pest management programs also are essential for maintaining quality. Deterrents from bird damage such as netting or hanging reflective material are often essential for fruit quality. Some farmers bag fruit on the tree in order to protect and enhance fruit

Ways to add value to crop quality

Pre-harvest	Harvest	Postharvest
Crop and variety selection	Perfect state of maturity	Follow recommended guidelines
Seed/plant quality	Proper technique for each crop	Stabilize (e.g., chill, dry, etc.) as soon as possible
Optimal growing environment	Minimize damage	Develop optimal practices for each operation
Crop protection		Shortest time to market
Crop management		

Craig Elevitch and Ken Love

quality (e.g., banana, lychee, loquat). To obtain the high quality fruit (e.g., mangos, lychee), fruit thinning is carried out on immature fruit to remove misshapen fruit and balance the number of leaves to each fruit, ensuring adequate fruit nutrient supply. Culling fruit at each step of the way to maximize top grade produce is another promotional tool for marketing what you produce. Pruning also facilitates harvesting and stimulates consistent fruiting.

Harvest

Harvesting at the perfect stage of maturity for a given end use is crucial for high-end markets. For example, a fully mature (but not quite ripe) mango has the best color, aroma, flavor, and sugar content. A common and inexpensive way to help track plant health and fruit quality/ripeness is through the use of a refractometer, which measures dissolved sugars (brix) in the juice or plant sap. Often farmers harvest too early (prior to full maturity) in order to increase shelf life or allow for distribution time to the customer. A better approach to maintain optimal quality is to minimize the time between harvesting and delivering to the customer or processing. Most fruits should be harvested directly into clean containers that are of an appropriate size and depth to avoid bruising. As common sense would dictate, allowing fruit to drop onto the ground during harvest should be eliminated.

Proper harvesting protocols should be followed for each crop. Avocados, for example, should be harvested with the stem attached, rather than removed, to greatly increase shelf life (the stem is later cut flush with the skin, but not removed). Certain customers, such as those making displays in restaurants, will pay a premium to have fruit with a small number of leaves still attached to the stem (e.g., mango, citrus, longan, etc.). Some fruits require additional handling during harvest. For example, breadfruit contains sticky latex sap. Cutting a breadfruit or jackfruit stem close to the skin and placing each fruit stem oriented downward to drain the latex for 30–60 minutes makes for an almost latex-free fruit in the kitchen.

It is also advisable to chill crops during the harvest if possible, or as soon after harvest as possible. For example, harvesting small fruits directly into protec-

Harvesting breadfruit when it is fully mature (two fruits on left) will yield the best eating quality, whereas immature fruit (right) will have a spongy, vegetable-like texture and little taste. Harvesting at the correct time takes more care, but results in a better product that customers prefer.

tive clamshell containers in a cooler with ice packs maximizes the shelf life of the crop and helps eliminate bruising by avoiding multiple handling steps and maintains moisture, nutrition and taste. In cases where washing and sorting are unnecessary, the field-cooled containers are ready for sale without further handling.

Postharvest

Postharvest treatment and handling practices prepare crops for immediate sale, processing, or storage for later use. Properly done, these practices help maintain or increase crop quality, safeguard food safety, and minimize losses. Poorly done, they reduce the value of the crop and ensure low prices in the marketplace, and, at worst, loss of the crop and invested production inputs. Therefore, planning an operation around good postharvest practices is an essential part of a value-added operation.

Each type of crop and end use has its own specific postharvest practices that need to be learned and adapted to each farm. Efficiency of postharvest processing design is important to maximize capacity and minimize handling. When adding crops, those that are handled and processed in the same way will not require additional infrastructure development, which helps keep down the cost of production.

Washing and cooling lettuce immediately after harvesting in South Kona.

Recommended postharvest treatment and handling procedures have been developed for most crops through extensive research by university programs throughout the world, including University of Hawai'i, and are a good starting point for optimizing on-farm practices. Practical recommendations for many fruit and vegetable crops can be found at Gross et al (2004). Avoiding mechanical damage, high temperature exposure and microbial and disease contamination is essential for all crops. In general, postharvest treatments include all steps from harvest to the consumer including (Kitinoja and Kader 2003)

- Transportation/handling—should be done in such a way to minimize bruising or other injury, maintain temperature and ventilation

- Cleaning—includes washing, brushing, air blowing, etc., depending on the crop

- Sorting—often done just after harvesting to sort out blemished or rotting produce and group into various grades by size, color, and stage of maturity.

- Curing—certain root, tuber and bulb crops are held at high temperature and relative humidity to allow healing of harvesting injuries, thereby increasing storage life

- Packing and packaging materials—protect harvested materials from damage and allow for some air circulation

- Decay and insect control—carried out through environmental control, cold or heat treatments, oxygen exclusion, pest control, and other methods

- Temperature, relative humidity, and light control—maintains quality in storage by reducing respiration and rate of water loss

- Food safety practices—elimination of postharvest problems that arise from physical and chemical hazards and human pathogens.

Example: Japanese Market

In Japan and many other countries, product quality is the primary "added-value" customers are seeking and for which they are willing to pay top price. Meticulous attention to detail is paid at every stage of cultivation. Sometimes colored bags are put over fruit or certain vegetables while they are growing in order to obtain a specific color shade and to prolong the growing time so that more sugars can develop naturally. Often photos of the farmers accompany in-store displays as an indicator of the pride put into the crop.

Optimal crop quality references

CTAHR Good Agricultural Practices Coaching: www.manoa.hawaii.edu/ctahr/farmfoodsafety/

Grades and standards, phytosanitary regulations: www.ams.usda.gov

INPhO, the Information Network on Post-harvest Operations: www.fao.org/inpho/en/

Postharvest Technology Research and Information Center: www.postharvest.org

PROCESSING

For the purposes of this guide, processing refers to any activity that brings raw products closer to consumption through a range of basic and advanced methods or techniques. The most basic processing techniques are covered above in "Postharvest" including, cleaning, sorting, grading, and packaging for storage. Processing can be much more advanced than these methods, ranging from simple extractions, to fermentation, to topical lotions, to finished culinary dishes.

Craig Elevitch and Ken Love

Coffee quality depends upon careful growing, harvesting, and postharvest handling. It begins with variety selection for the region and ideal growing conditions and nutrition. Harvesting only fully mature beans, then carefully fermenting (or demucilaging), drying, milling, and grading. Finally, a perfect roast and brew will yield the highest value cup of coffee.

The art and science of processing and preserving locally grown foods is potentially one of the most worthwhile undertakings of a small farm enterprise in Hawai'i. Potential rewards include increased profits, developing unique products for unique markets, and the satisfaction of following one's passions. The challenges are also substantial, including time and capital investments in product development and the risks associated with uncertain supply and consumer demand.

Processing is the backbone of value-added in Hawai'i not only because it creates unique products that are differentiated in the marketplace, but also because processed products capture a higher percentage of the retail price. Developing, processing and selling a value-added product can determine how profitable or sustainable a small farm enterprise can be. Using coffee as an example again, the relative dollar value of a cup of coffee compared with freshly harvested coffee cherry (with production losses accounted for) is 7:1 by weight (Smith et al 2011). In other words, seven times the income can be derived from selling a brewed cup of coffee compared with selling coffee cherry. This comparison is not a measure of profit, because the costs of processing, serving, etc., are not included, however, it does indicate that most of the value of a brewed cup of coffee is derived through processing.

Planning for processing

Processing requires developing new skills and usually acquiring new facilities and equipment. Certain types of processing have been developed over centuries, such as processing tea, which is an artisan skill requiring years of training and experience. Other processing is relatively simple, requiring only off-the-shelf equipment and a short training period. In all cases, research into various methods is essential to ensure an efficient operation that produces the desired results and a highly competitive product based on cost and quality. In many cases the costs of processing a product outweighs reasonable expected returns, in which case careful planning can preclude failure. Processing equipment and training can be such a large investment that hiring an expert in processing a specific product may be advisable, saving costs in the long run.

Often gaining a competitive advantage requires "thinking outside the box," or developing value-added products that are obtainable within a given resource budget (time, money, capital). What would differentiate a farm's coffee from that of hundreds of competing farms? Perhaps uniquely flavored coffees packaged with locally grown cinnamon or orange peel might strike a chord with certain visitor groups. Ready-to-use coffee extracts might be developed to satisfy market demand from more health-conscious customers. In any case, it can require a substantial amount of research to make a product that stands out and can be sold at a fair market price for a profit.

Generic processing categories

This table lists various processing methods and processed products that add value to a generic commodity. Each of these requires training and experience to develop a quality product.

Baked goods	Culinary dishes	Lotions, creams	Flavored foods (spiced nuts, etc.)	Jams, jellies, chutneys
Drinks (brewed, mixed, etc.)	Prepared foods (chocolate, ice cream, etc.)	Flavorings (spice mixes, sauces, dressings, etc.)	Candying (fruit and nuts)	Roasting
Artificially preserving (can, jar, pouch)	Milling (flour, powders)	Juicing	Refining	Crafts (Fiber and wood products)
Extracting (tincture, hydrosol, distilled)	Extracting (press, expeller, solvent)	Cutting, peeling	Freezing	Sawing/milling (wood products)
Partially cooking	Fermenting	Pickling	Curing (salting, smoking)	Drying
Treated for export	Cleaning	Polishing, waxing	Grading	Sorting

Many processing activities require a certified kitchen or processing facility, both of which necessitate a substantial capital investment and a range of government permits (Department of Health, Planning Department, Fire Department, etc.). The scope of requirements for a certified kitchen can vary based on anticipated processing methods and region within Hawai'i. Municipal water supply may be required, and this can be a challenge in areas using only catchment water. Many have found that the requirements are a moving target and that they can change without warning, even during the construction of a previously approved facility. A cost-effective alternative to building a costly certified kitchen is to rent time in a privately or community owned facility.

For all forms of processing, there are a plethora of applicable local and national laws. Often confusing and contradictory, they must be carefully researched. In Hawai'i, laws regarding food safety, where certain processed foods can be prepared and sold, and local permitting policies vary from island to island and sometimes between regions on an island. Navigating applicable laws can be disheartening, but well worth the time and effort to avoid future costs to retrofit an operation. National laws, which take precedence over state laws, apply to a range of processed foods and alcoholic beverages. See the "Resources" section for a list of organizations that can lend assistance.

Example: Preserving

Even before agriculture, food preservation was developed of necessity and for survival. Today food preservation such as canning, drying, fermenting and pickling are done for future use and in case of emergency. Done carefully, food preservation also converts perishable crops into safe products with a long shelf life that a small producer can sell at a profit to increase financial viability. In many cases, such as canning or preserving, specific parameters must be adhered to in order to ensure the product is safe in the long-term. Programs such as the Master Food Preservers certified training, which is conducted throughout the United States, teach basic food safety and a variety of techniques employed to safely preserve foods.

Perhaps the most common preserved foods seen in local farmers markets are jams and jellies made from fruit, spices and other produce items. A key to safety with jams and jellies is a pH (acidity) below 4.6, mixture of the processed fruit, sugar and pectin in the appropriate order, and then boiling for 20 minutes in sterilized jars. There are a number of variables, especially with tropical fruit. For example, lilikoi or passion fruit, jaboticaba, guava and many others might usually need only 40% sugar, but at times require up to 60% sugar in order to achieve an acceptable sweetness. To achieve a safe product pH for certain crops such as tomato, papaya or fig, extra

Craig Elevitch and Ken Love

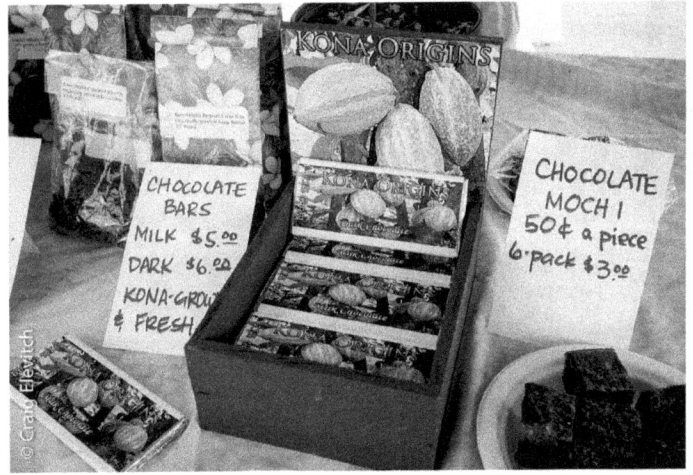

Processing is an art that requires acquiring skills and experience. Chocolate, for example, goes through many stages from bean to bar, including fermentation, drying/roasting, conching (milling) with other ingredients, tempering, and forming.

acidity (from vinegar or lemon) may be required in order for canning to be safe. High pressure canning requires a pressure canner, different from a pressure cooker. The canner can accurately measure the pressure inside when preserving meats, fish, poultry and low-acid vegetables such as beans. Building up pressure heats water to 121°C (250°F), which is hot enough to kill spores that cause botulism.

Pickling and fermentation are other ancient forms of preservation that take on different forms in different cultures and ethnicity. Miso and fermented soybeans (*natto*) in Japan, sauerkraut in Germany, kim chee in Korea, and fermented fish in Scandinavia are examples. Fermented sodas, beers and wine are also fermented foods.

Having a product made with fresh, local ingredients appeals to certain customers, who will be willing to pay more for it than similar inexpensive imported products. Additionally, a product made with all natural ingredients and without synthetic chemical ingredients with unpronounceable names is a big plus when explaining the value of your product to consumers. Continually striving for exceptional flavor and other qualities determines the long term success of the product.

Processing references

Elevitch, C.R. (ed.) 2011. Specialty Crops for Pacific Islands. Permanent Agriculture Resources, Holualoa. www.agroforestry.net/scps

University of California Home Preservation and Storage Publications: www.ucfoodsafety.ucdavis.edu/ UC_Publications/UC_Home_Preservation_and_Storage_Publications/

The National Center for Home Food Preservation: http://nchfp.uga.edu

USDA's Food storage and preservation: http://fnic.nal.usda.gov/consumers/all-about-food/food-storage-and-preservation

Value added and processing: https://attra.ncat.org/marketing.html#valueadded

Packaging

Packaging is the physical container that is used to portion out, protect, transport, store, and sell a product. Product information is also printed on or affixed to the packaging and is covered under "Labeling" below. How a value-added product is packaged plays a key role in sales to different markets. The importance of quality in selling applies to the raw agricultural product, the processed products produced from it, and, equally important, the packaging. It does not matter if the package contents are far superior to competing versions, if the presentation or packaging is unattractive, inappropriate, or impractical, customers will fail to appreciate the added value.

The art of packaging involves beauty and functionality, while the science of packaging involves materials and chemistry. Generally, for value-added products, the artfulness of the packaging (and labeling) receives much greater emphasis than for mainstream products. The packaging must correspond to the real and perceived value of the product to the intended customer. For example, high-end jams and jellies

Several brands of Hawaiian honey in various types of plastic and glass packaging. Each type (material, size, dispensing style) appeals to certain customer preferences and carries its own costs and benefits.

are sold at retail in attractive clear glass jars, rather than plastic jars. Glass allows the customer to judge the contents by color and texture while also serving as an airtight container for long-term storage. An unusual or custom jar will further differentiate preserves from other products on the market, although the costs of custom packaging may be too high for a small-scale operation.

One must also consider separate packaging for different types of customers. Package size and materials may be different for retail, wholesale, chef, service industry, grocery store, gift items or home consumption. Household size jars of jam will probably not appeal to restaurants, for example, and large jars are costly and impractical, so another attractive and functional bulk packaging must be used. Very small sample jars may be ideal for sampler packs or for visitors who are looking for lightweight, affordable gifts.

Packaging cost can also be a large factor in choosing materials and portion size. For example, custom packaging can differentiate a product, but the value added to the product may be less than the custom manufactured packaging. In Hawai'i, packaging costs are especially high because most packaging materials must be shipped from the continental U.S. For small farm operations, custom labeling may be the only economically feasible way to customize the product appearance. It is often a wise investment to hire a packaging consultant to help develop packag-

ing for a product line that is best suited for customer needs, while minimizing costs for a Hawai'i processor.

Example: Packaging for Japanese visitor market

When catering to the Japanese visitor market in Hawai'i, it is wise to pay close attention to packaging and sizing requirements and preferences. Stories of value-added product failure in Japan because of poor packaging are legendary to those in the business of marketing in the country.

Sizing and portions are very different in Japan compared with the U.S. An obvious difference is metric sizing, which is used in Japan (and nearly all countries). The portion size should be researched carefully to match the Japanese expectations for a particular product. The quantity of items is also important to Japanese customers. For example, there are often five items to a package, not four (one of the words for four also means death). Often, especially for gift items, the physical packaging is shaped like the produce it contains, e.g., pineapple cookies in a bag shaped like and printed with a picture of a pineapple. Japanese also use layers of packaging, e.g., an outer wrapping, a box, and an inner wrapping. Packaging for gifts and *omiyage* for Japanese customers is an art and science that should be carefully studied before attempting to enter that market or other foreign markets.

Packaging for Japanese and other foreign visitors to Hawai'i should be carefully researched to meet the expectations of those specific markets.

Craig Elevitch and Ken Love

Packaging references

USDA Ag Marketing Resource Center: www.agmrc.org

Labeling

Labeling consists of written and graphical communications on or associated with packaging. Although repeat sales and referrals depend upon actual product quality, value, consistency and service, often the packaging and labeling lead to the first sale. Because labeling usually gives the initial impression to customers, it is one of the most important aspects of value-added.

State and federal laws (and those of other countries and international law for exports) regulate the content and size of labels. Most packaged goods in Hawai'i are required to meet labeling guidelines, while certain other categories such as raw produce and fish, bulk items, certain small-scale operations, and food for immediate consumption are exempt. The core concepts underlying U.S. Federal labeling laws are that the label must be truthful and not mislead the consumer. For specific and current requirements for product labeling, it is highly recommended to consult with the Hawai'i Department of Health Food and Drug Branch. Along with the labeling requirements, value-added operations should make optimal use of labeling as a marketing tool while adhering to applicable laws.

Often the label is the first thing that the customer notices. The package attracts the eye and the label holds the interest—together they sell the product. When the interplay of color, shapes, design, and text font and size strike a responsive chord with potential customers, they will take more than a passing interest in the product. For some products, keeping the label very simple is best, for others, extensive details or explanations might be needed, at least until the product is established in the marketplace. For example, descriptions for exotic fruit and unusual vegetables are often needed for mainland and overseas customers in Hawai'i.

Choosing what labeling is best for a product and target markets takes time and forethought, especially for a unique product. A good place to begin conceptualizing is to look at labels for similar products at various retail locations. Possibilities range from simple handmade labels to those that cost thousands to design—both appeal to different customers.

The next step is to create some design mock-ups and ask friends and trusted associates what they think. Some companies have introduced products and changed the label multiple times in order to find which labeling works best for which markets. Pro-

Labeling content

Mandatory (consult federal guidelines for complete list)	Non-mandatory (potentially add value)
Product name (common or usual name)	Product information and benefits
Net content (volume or weight)	Images (accurate portrayals)
Ingredient statement	Producer introduction
Allergen information	Origin (Hawai'i grown, region where grown, etc.)
Responsibility statement (name, address)	Certifications (organic certification agency, food safety, GMO free, etc.)
Nutrition Facts	Nutritional benefits (as per applicable law)
Country of origin (when imported to U.S.)	Manufacturing date*
Producer location	"Best before" date*
	Universal Product Code (UPC)*
	Product batch code or lot number*
	Web site, social media information
	QR code (for URL link to web page)
	Producer contact information
	Other languages (depending on market)

* Required by food distributors and retailers

Labeling of fresh fruits and vegetables is not required, however, a sticker identifying the farm and any certifications, as well as other product information can add significant value to a product. Also, signage at the point of sale informing potential customers about cultivation practices, special characteristics of the product, and identifying the producer can also greatly increase the value to customers and the price they are willing to pay.

fessional help is a wise investment once a product is ready for larger markets.

Labeling varies depending on the market. A different label for the same product is often employed to differentiate markets. Often the package size might determine differences in labeling. For example, a larger label on a bulk size container that states "Food Service" will be of more interest to chefs than small quantities.

Specifically targeting markets in labeling can help add value. For example, a number of coffee farmers in Hawai'i have multiple labels for the same product, such as for special occasions like birthdays, Valentine's Day, or New Year celebrations. Private labels made to order for retailers or even individual customers can also increase sales. Using languages in addition to English (required by law) makes a huge difference for visitor and export markets. Expecta-

tions for package imagery vary from culture to culture. For example, Asian markets show a picture of the main product ingredients. From chewing gum to expensive brandy, if it is made with a fruit, that fruit is depicted on the label.

Labeling references

FDA labeling guidelines: www.fda.gov/Food/GuidanceComplianceRegulatoryInformation/GuidanceDocuments/FoodLabelingNutrition/default. htm

State of Hawai'i Department of Agriculture coffee labeling guidelines: www.hawaii.gov/hdoa/aad-comm/coffee

State of Hawai'i Department of Health. 2009 (revised). Basic Guidelines for Food Labeling. Food and Drug Branch, Honolulu.

USDA Ag Marketing Resource Center: www.agmrc. org

Craig Elevitch and Ken Love

Comparing basic labeling (left) and more professional labeling (right) for value-added moringa products shows the impact of attractive and informative labels. A professionally designed label makes most products much more appealing and engages potential customers in learning more about and appreciating the product.

Branding

Branding identifies a producer's goods and services through names, design, graphics and other features of labeling, packaging, and advertising. Product identification reflects on and mirrors the producer's farm or processing location, the farm or company identity and history, as well as telling stories that help customers better understand the company and its products. Regional associations and ethnic heritage (e.g., Hawaiian) are also used for branding and marketing goods or services. By building a unique identity for the producer, good branding potentially adds value to the producer's entire product line, including innovative products that are unfamiliar to customers.

Branding involves significant thought and planning, including company and product names, logo, and the personality of text and imagery. It is costly and time consuming to change these once they have been established. As with many aspects of running a business, it is often a good investment to hire a professional to help develop a brand identity.

Branding of value-added products should tie into the product strengths for given markets. For example, a locally grown, handcrafted traditional food product such as taro poi should have a brand that resonates with the core customer base for this type of product. Thinking ahead from the outset to a diversified product line is wise. For a small company with limited resources, having a common identity across a product line seems to work best. If a customer prefers a company's taro poi, they will be more likely to buy other related products from that company. In other words, a company's reputation can add value to future product offerings by association with a brand. A natural product line to complement taro poi might be 'ulu poi, taro corms and ti leaves, and prepared lau lau—all of these potential products can be included in the brand from the outset even though only one product will be sold for the first few years.

How one uses branding to differentiate a product from others depends upon the product strengths that are emphasized for a given market. For instance, high-end chefs look for reliability, freshness, and su-

Each of these three Hawai'i Island companies has developed its own brand identity, emphasizing their unique product strengths.

Example brand associations

Reputable and recognizable family name
Desirable region
Product characteristics (e.g., locally grown)
Product certifications (e.g., organic, food safety)
Healthy lifestyles
Nutrition
Community/cultural associations

perior taste and appearance, all of which should be embodied in its logo and product descriptions by a company that targets this market. Customers looking for organic produce are probably also concerned about non-biodegradable packaging, so it makes sense for an organic farm to package in biodegradable or easily recyclable materials. In short, branding should always play to product strengths in the minds of customers.

CERTIFICATIONS AND REPUTATION

Independent certifications and testimonials can go a long way in differentiating locally produced, artisan products from mainstream counterparts and in many cases increase the price customers are willing to spend. Agricultural, product, and regional certifications require compliance with a specific set of standards, documentation and record keeping, and usually regular site inspections. Example certifications are listed in the table below.

The relatively young coffee industry in Kaʻū is developing its own brand that is already identified with quality thanks to good marketing and high scores in international competitions.

Each certification has its own costs in terms of time, resources, and fees, and its own benefits in terms of the value customers place on them. Studies comparing certified organic with non-organic food show that the price premium for organic is usually below 30%, although in certain cases it can be much more, even exceeding 100% (USDA ERS 2012). Looking at prices for comparable products with and without a certain certification label can indicate the price premium one can expect. For unique products with no competition, the price premium one can expect can be difficult to estimate. Small enterprises that sell directly to customers often see the extra work of independent certification as a hassle with questionable value. Instead, they educate their customers directly through product descriptions, advertising, and one-on-one conversations. For many customers, the trust built through direct customer interactions with producers exceeds the value any third-party certification could add.

Food safety certification is increasingly becoming important to customers, especially for larger producers. Many wholesalers currently require food safety certification, and this requirement is expected to become universal. Because certification can require high expenditures for infrastructure, small farm enterprises may not initially be able to justify the cost. However, all farm operations should closely follow Good Agricultural Practices (GAPs), a set of guidelines that are the basis for food safety certification. Some smaller wholesale and retail customers are willing to establish a relationship with a farmer who has a demonstrated commitment to following GAPs backed by regular producer updates and customer site visits. Free or low cost basic food safety training and testing (e.g., www.hifoodhandlers.com) is a convenient way to learn about food safety. Although not yet required in Hawaiʻi, most states require such a program for all food handlers and farmers market vendors.

Source designation

"Locally grown" food has become an effective selling point as consumers become increasingly committed to supporting the local food economy wherever they are (at home or travelling). "Made in Hawaiʻi" and "Product of Hawaiʻi" are designations that can

Craig Elevitch and Ken Love

Example third-party certifications

Farm and processing methods	USDA Organic, Biodynamic®, Food Alliance, Certified Naturally Grown, Hawai'i Seals of Quality
Business practices	Fair Trade USA, Food Justice Certification
Environmental benefits	Bird Friendly® (coffee), Rainforest Alliance Certified
Food Safety	Food Safety Certified

be used for any product for which "at least fifty-one per cent of its wholesale value added by manufacture, assembly, fabrication, or production within the State" (HRS §486-119). Unfortunately, this definition presents a low standard, as inexpensive imported ingredients or products can easily constitute 49% or less of a products wholesale value once sold

Example: Japanese Market

Japanese consumers are rather exacting when it comes to quality. Not only does the product have to be top quality, but its inner and outer packaging and labeling all have to be perfect. Quality and consistency are absolutely required in developing a sustainable business for the Japanese market. You must have repeat customers with a business that spreads by word of mouth.

Examples of third party certifications that can add value to products.

in Hawai'i. Many consumers are confused by this, thinking that "Made in Hawai'i" means grown and processed in Hawai'i. As more consumers become aware of this deceptive labeling practice, it is wise to state which ingredients are locally grown on the label, e.g., "Made from 100% Hawaiian-grown macadamia nuts." "Made in USA" has a much higher standard than the Hawai'i State designation—it applies only where "all or virtually all" of the product has been made in the U.S.

Additional local source designations include "Made in Maui," "Kaua'i Made," and "Moloka'i Made in Hawai'i," which are to be used only for products from their respective islands. A special source designation exists for "Kona Coffee," which by law can only be used to describe coffee grown within the North and South Kona districts of Hawai'i Island. All of these legally defined source designations may increase the perceived value, and many of them require little effort and expense to obtain.

Testimonials and awards

Customer statements praising a product or company bolster product and company reputation. The more authoritative or distinguished the source, the more valuable the testimonial. Awards given for product quality carry great weight in a customer's mind, especially those won in large, open national and international competitions.

Product certification references

Codex Alimentarius, International Food Standards: www.codexalimentarius.org

Fair Trade USA: www.fairtradeusa.org

Food safety extension publications at UH: www.ctahr.hawaii.edu/hnfas/publications.html

Hawai'i Department of Agriculture Seals of Quality Program: www.hawaii.gov/hdoa/add/soq

Example regional marks in Hawaiʻi.

Hawaiʻi Organic Farmers Association: www.hawaiiorganic.org

International Portal on Food Safety, Animal and Plant Health (IPFSAPH): www.ipfsaph.org/En/

Pacific Agrosecurity & Food Safety Program of the University of Hawaiʻi: www.manoa.hawaii.edu/ctahr/pacific-afsp/?page_id=127

Rangarajan, A., E.A. Bihn, R.B. Gravani, D.L. Scott, and M.P. Pritts. 2000. Food Safety Begins on the Farm: A Grower's Guide. Cornell University, Ithaca, New York. www.gaps.cornell.edu/Educational-materials/Samples/FSBFEngMED.pdf

CUSTOMER SERVICE

Customer service can greatly add to the value of a product line, often at nominal cost. In general, customers who buy value-added, locally produced products are interested in having a closer relationship with their food than what they can get from mainstream products. They want to know that they are having a positive impact on their community and that they are purchasing a higher quality and more nutritious product than they can get elsewhere. Customers also expect reliability, consistency, and accountability from small vendors at a standard equal to or better than offered by large corporations.

Reliability

Reliability engenders a sense of trust both in the producer and the products. Keeping agreements with customers can be as simple as delivering a product with consistent quality, on time, every time, or as complex as fulfilling a contract to produce and deliver a special order. In many cases, retailers or restaurants can be greatly inconvenienced or can risk losing customers when a vendor fails to follow through as expected. If a product becomes temporarily unavailable due to weather, for example, it is best to inform customers as soon as possible that there will be a gap in supply. Reliability is a strong asset that adds value to a small farm enterprise—customers will often pay more for the goods provided by a reliable supplier.

Consistency

Many will buy a product once. However, repeat sales should be a primary business goal. This can only happen with product consistency, which should be a primary focus for anyone producing value-added products, especially in Hawaiʻi's tourist-based economy where survival might depend upon repeat internet or mail order purchases. The first time a product fails to meet quality expectations is often the last

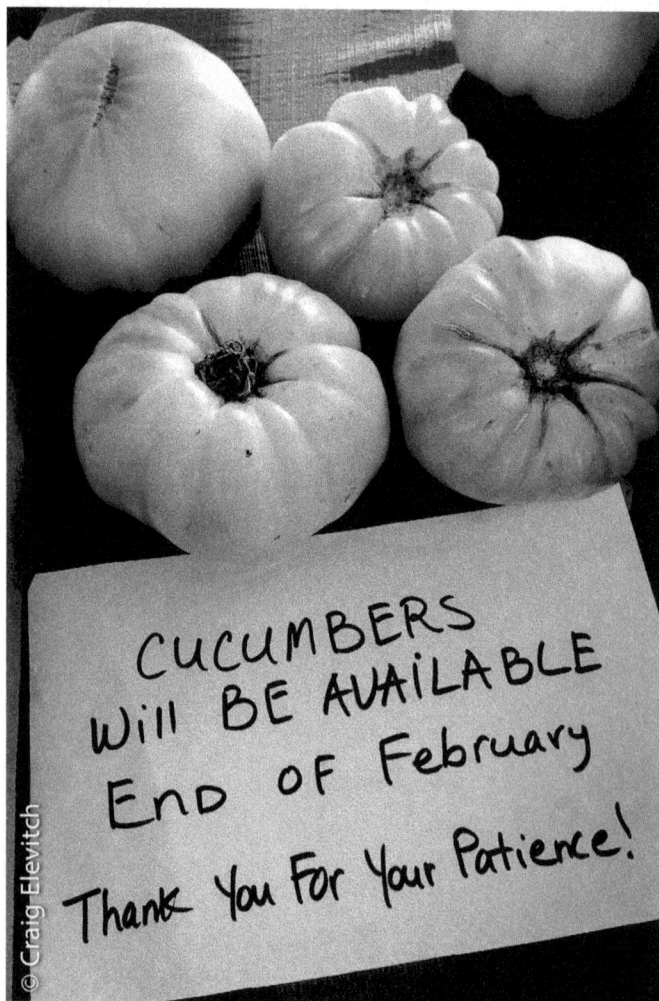

Keeping customers continually informed is an essential part of customer service.

time a customer will buy it. While a disruption may put off customers, some will understand and appreciate the situation and will remain loyal, especially if they are kept updated.

Cultivate relationships with customers

Courteous and friendly interaction goes a long way toward building lasting customer relationships. Direct sales opportunities at farmers markets, on-farm sales locations, and at special events are perfect opportunities to talk with customers. A regular personal telephone call to check in with larger customers can help strengthen relationships and provide crucial information for product improvements and diversification. Social media and email offer valuable opportunities to interact with customers—it is important to respond quickly and courteously to all messages through electronic media to give customers a sense that "someone is home" and actively running the business. Soliciting product feedback (without arguing with it) gives customers a sense that they play an important role in the success of their supplier's business. Respond to customer feedback by refining a product or connected service and adapt to current market conditions.

Guarantee

Simply put, an unconditional money back guarantee tells customers that you care and that they can trust the product. This can be important to new customers, especially when the product cost is significantly higher than other options. For a high quality, honestly represented, and consistent product, the rate of product return or loss claims should be low—the cost of these claims will be included in the cost of production.

PRICING

Setting prices is a balancing act between an amount that is high enough to cover the cost of production and reasonable profits, and prices that do not exceed comparable mainstream products by too much. As noted in the "Introduction," calculating the cost of production sets the bottom line for pricing. Cost of production includes labor, materials, capital, subcontracted costs, and overhead, in other words, all cash and non-cash costs associated with production, selling and marketing. A time consuming but worthwhile practice is to keep a log of all time and expenses associated with a product for a year. This process will give a realistic record of the true costs involved. Selling below the cost of production is not sustainable. Many farmers fail to include their labor, office expenses and physical infrastructure costs in their budget in the hopes of remaining price-competitive. These are real costs that must be compensated and recognized. Farmers who subsidize their products by setting prices below the cost of production are usually hobbyists who do not need to earn a living from their products or they soon go out of business.

An accurate cost of production is a starting point for setting prices. The next step is usually to survey the marketplace to determine current prices for comparable products, both mainstream versions and local value-added, where they exist. If market prices are too low compared to the cost of production, this may indicate that the product will not be viable or needs to be changed in order to make it profitable. However, if market prices are above the cost of production, this is an indicator that a value-added product can be successful. If customers perceive they are getting their money's worth from a quality product, they are more likely to return for more.

Obviously there are many factors to consider when setting prices in addition to the cost of production, e.g., availability, seasonality, competition, and a va-

Responsive and friendly customer service greatly increases customer satisfaction and goes hand-in-hand with a value-added farm business.

Pricing must not only cover the cost of production and reasonable profit, but must also reflect the value perceived by the customer.

most successful businesses sell their products to different markets at a range of price points.

The formula 30%-30%-30% is a general guide to pricing for wholesale, retailer, and direct sales, respectively. For example, if the cost of production is $10.00, the price (in large quantity) for a wholesaler will be about $13.00, or a 30% mark-up. The wholesaler will then add their 30% mark-up for their customers (retailers and restaurants) for a price of $16.90. The retailer will then add their 30% mark-up and sell the product at retail ($22.00) or the chef will use it in some culinary creation, which again sells at roughly retail. This pricing guide is a good general starting place for pricing. However, there are a number of caveats and variations to these guidelines, such as gourmet stores and exclusive locations, for example, that usually have much higher mark-ups.

riety of other factors. Competition can be a governing consideration when competing closely with imported products. For example, a 150 ml (5 oz) jar of guava jelly costs about $2.60 to produce in Hawai'i but only $0.50 if imported to Honolulu from Malaysia or Thailand. This makes it extremely hard to compete based on price, especially when both jars can be marked "Made in Hawai'i." However, several brands of locally grown and processed jams and jellies are profitable in Hawai'i because their products are fresher and more flavorful and are marketed to the right customers. For these customers, $5–10 for a small jar of high quality preserves is acceptable.

Setting a low price in order to undercut other vendors may mistakenly indicate to customers that the product really is the same as other generic or imported products. Prices should be set at a level commensurate with the real and perceived value. This is an area where setting a higher price than for generic comparable products actually does add value to the product.

Pricing by market

There are essentially two approaches to making money from value-added products: sell a limited quantity at a high price with a large mark-up or sell a large quantity at a low price with a small mark-up. The first approach usually consists of direct sales at retail, while the second relies upon wholesaling. Both methods can be successful and profitable only after careful analysis of the marketplace and production capacity. As covered in the "Markets" section below,

Following general guidelines for pricing for wholesalers and retailers can help ensure that there is room for everyone to make money from a product.

Craig Elevitch and Ken Love

MARKETS

According to the USDA Economic Research Service Food Dollar Series (2011), farmers receive about 16 cents on average for every consumer dollar spent on food. The remaining 84 cents of the consumer food dollar goes toward processing, packaging, transportation, retail mark-up, food services, and other overhead expenses. A successful value-added operation includes ways to earn a higher percentage of the consumer food dollar compared with selling generic products to wholesalers and processors.

The term "market" refers to a group of buyers with common interests and requirements. General market categories include wholesale distributors, processors, retailers, restaurants, and consumers. Each market requires a certain product volume, pricing, packaging, delivery frequency, quality standard, and so on. Selling to several of these markets, where feasible and profitable, is essential for the success of a small farm enterprise in Hawai'i.

Market diversity

Although it may be very tempting to plan on selling only to the highest value markets such as directly to consumers and high-end restaurants, most successful farm businesses sell to customers in a variety of markets. There are many reasons to diversify markets. First, it is logistically difficult for a small farm enterprise to reach all potential customers through direct sales. Selling in quantity to a grocery store or wholesaler greatly expands the customer base, even though the income derived is considerably less per unit compared with direct sales. Also, wider sales through retail and wholesale channels raise awareness about a farm's products and can increase demand from other markets, e.g., directly from consumers. Second, there are often periods of an oversupply, usually due to the seasonality of crops, but also for other reasons. Having a strong, consistent relationship with a wholesaler allows the sale of large quantities when available—this can reduce lost sales opportunities during heavy production periods. Third, having different markets allows selling all consumable grades of produce. For example, first quality produce can be sold at its highest value to consumers and retailers, slightly blemished or irregular produce can be sold to certain restaurants or at the farmers

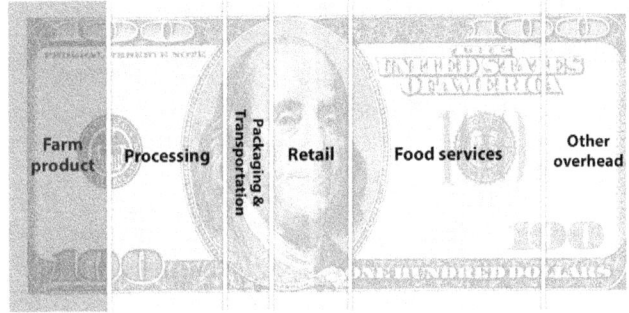

Farmers receive for their raw commodity an average about 16% of the dollar consumers spend on food. (Illustration adapted from USDA ERS 2011.)

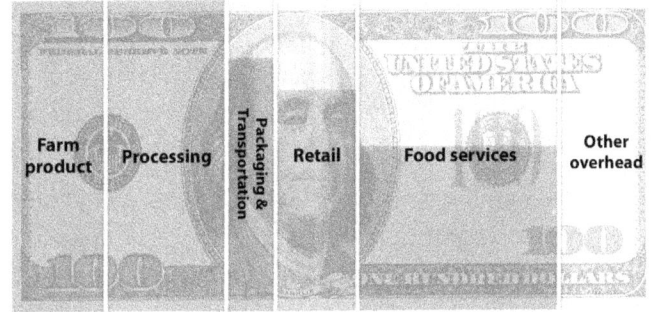

In addition to the value of their raw food commodity, farmers who process, distribute, sell directly to retail customers and consumers, and/or sell ready-to-eat food can earn a much larger portion of the consumer food dollar. (Illustration adapted from USDA ERS 2011.)

market, and off-grade produce can be processed. Fourth, market diversity allows a farm enterprise to better withstand changes in the marketplace due to competition, market changes (e.g., loss of a farmers market), and policy fluctuations. In other words, diversity reduces the inherent risks of doing business in a small number of venues. Finally, some markets are a better match for a farm enterprise than others due to product line, producer personality, location, and so on. A diversity of markets helps determine what work best and is the most profitable; the best combination of markets can be emphasized in future product development.

Markets references

Elevitch, C., N. Milne, and J. Cain. 2012. Hawai'i Island Farmer's Guide to Accessing Local Markets. HCC OCET, Center for Agricultural Success, and PAR. www.hawaiihomegrown.net/pdfs/Hawaii-Island-Guide-to-Accessing-Markets.pdf

Business Action Center market research links: www.hawaii.gov/dcca/bac/research.html

USDA Ag Marketing Resource Center: www.agmrc.org

EXAMPLE VALUE-ADDED ENTERPRISES

In 2012, the Agribusiness Incubator Program of the University of Hawai'i selected the following twelve Hawai'i-based agricultural enterprises as exemplary producers from a pool of 45 applicants to their value-added grant program. Selection criteria included growth potential, positive impact on Hawai'i agriculture, product innovation, and the successful track records of the companies.

Voyaging Foods, Hawai'i Kai, O'ahu

Brynn Foster, owner
www.voyagingfoods.com

Brynn Foster started her personal voyage to develop healthy food products from indigenous Hawaiian crops in 2005. As a young mother, she was dedicated to finding healthy foods for her children. Motivated by a lack of commercially available teething biscuits free from refined sugar, diary, and gluten, Foster's first product was a taro-based teething biscuit.

"Growing up, I knew how important taro and poi are as a baby's first food. I wanted to get taro into my children's diet in more ways than just poi, so I baked it and used it as a flour replacement," recounts Foster about her early years. "My college thesis at Pepperdine University was about the Hawaiian's physical and spiritual connection to the land, so I finally was able to apply what I studied and knew intellectually to something tangible." Through this process of discovery, Foster began her career as more than a food processor, but as a local food advocate.

There was a long learning period of seven years, during which time Foster learned about growing and processing taro. Inspired in many ways by the work of the Reppun 'ohana and Jerry Konanui, she gradually expanded her knowledge and appreciation for taro. Taro flour revealed itself as the most promising processed product for the product line and customer base that Foster envisioned, so she devoted herself to reading all the research material she could find about taro flour. She interviewed a range of university professors for their input. "I was really fascinated about why things didn't work out with taro products in the past. I heard that the economics of Hawaiian

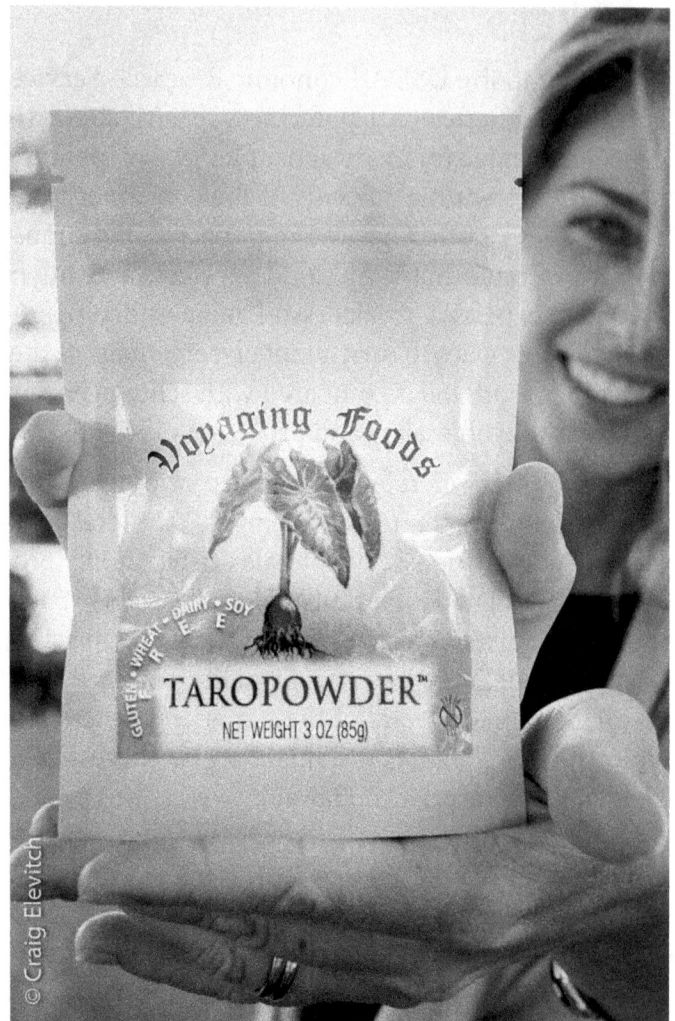

Brynn Foster of Voyaging Foods with one of her taro products, which are free from gluten, wheat, dairy, and soy.

taro and that consumer acceptance had been issues with commercialization previously." Partly because of Foster's Hawaiian ancestors, and partly because of her drive to support the local food system, her passion for taro goes far beyond profits.

Taro's time-tested nutritional value, combined with being gluten-free and hypoallergenic, has formed the basis for a product line that began with the teething biscuits and now includes ready-to-use taro flour, flakes, and pancake mix. These shelf-stable products are sold in Hawai'i and on the U.S. mainland, which the company currently reaches through their web site. Foster also has a wholesale bakery that uses her taro products in a range of baked goods including breads and energy bars sold through select local cafes and health food stores.

University of Hawai'i resource specialists that have helped and motivated Foster throughout the multiyear process of developing her business include the Agribusiness Incubator Program, Jim Hollyer of College of Tropical Agriculture and Human Resources, and Soojin Jun of the Department of Human Nutrition, Food and Animal Sciences.

Now that Foster has developed a product line and business model, her job is to educate customers about the products. "More and more people understand the value of gluten-free flours. My role now is to inform people about taro as a healthy food, how nutritious it is for body and spirit."

Hawaiian Chip Company, Kalihi Kai, Honolulu

Jimmy Chan, Owner
www.hawaiianchipcompany.com

Jimmy Chan went into business after graduating from college in 2000. After two important learning experiences with businesses that did not take off, Chan found success in his chip company, which is now 20 employees strong with distribution throughout Hawai'i. As his business grew, he found that focusing on product quality was the key to success in selling to bigger and better accounts. Every new account challenged him to continue maintaining quality, while a track record of high quality led to additional accounts.

Hawaiian Chip Company specializes in taro and sweetpotato chips. Quality begins with sourcing fresh Hawai'i-grown produce: taro from Hawai'i Island and Waialua, orange sweetpotato from Moloka'i, and purple sweetpotato from Hawai'i Island and Mililani. The company delivers its products directly to a range of specialty stores and supplies larger markets through big distributors. They ship Internet purchases directly to customers. Currently, the company does not have retail sales on the mainland U.S. due to limited raw materials and the inability to control inventory quality in distant locations.

Chan has recently developed a made-to-order chip retail outlet at his Kalihi Kai production facility. Customers can walk in or call in to order chips to be picked up still warm from the kitchen. Chan enthusiastically describes the new products, "Made-to-order chips provide a unique experience for consum-

© Craig Elevitch

Jimmy Chan of Hawaiian Chip Company at the company's retail location in Kalihi Kai, where customers can purchase made-to-order chips and flavor them to taste from the seasoning bar.

ers. Not only do they get to experience freshly made chips, but they can flavor the chips however they like from our seasoning bar." This unique experience and the quality products account for a significant portion of business coming from word-of-mouth advertising. "It's not just the products we offer that build connections with customers. When they come into our retail outlet, we welcome them warmly and acknowledge where they come from," explains Chan. Since the made-to-order chip business serves more adventurist customers, Chan caters to them by teaching them about the products and how they are made. Raw taro corms and sweetpotato tubers are on display so that customers can experience the Hawai'i-grown materials, how they are handled, and how much care is put into the product at each stage of the process. "The made-to-order chips give customers something to tell their friends and family. They can return to their family and say, 'I bought a bag of freshly made chips and seasoned it myself!' Such experiences are an important part of the brand we are building," says Chan.

In addition to word-of-mouth advertising, Hawaiian Chip Company educates new customers face-to-face at craft fairs and tradeshows, such as the Made in Hawai'i Festival. Giving people a chance to sample the product is important. For example, the purple sweetpotato chips are unfamiliar to many visitors and they have to try them before buying. Chan firmly believes, "Our product quality is built upon customer suggestions and feedback. We want to hear the good and the bad."

One of the biggest challenges that Chan has faced is to increase profits while maintaining quality. He invests his energy only on products that he is passionate about, which he believes is a key to success. Chan credits his value-added product achievements to keeping an open mind and learning from others at every opportunity, such as when travelling to new places or talking with other entrepreneurs. One inspiration for Chan has been hearing from Allen Ikawa about his experiences building Big Island Candies into a worldwide leader. "That company has set the standard for value-added—building up to that standard continually inspires me to get better. My philosophy is to add value to my products, then add value to that value—I'm always looking for ways add more value," says Chan.

Kahala FRESH, Kahala, Honolulu

Daryl E. Yamaguchi, co-owner
www.skahalafresh.com

Kahala FRESH is a start-up company that specializes in processing, packaging and distributing Hawai'i-grown produce. The company is an offshoot of the venerable Umeke Market of downtown Honolulu and is run by current and former associates of the market. The company specializes in Hawai'i-grown dried fruits, vegetables, nuts, and baked goods primarily for the visitor market.

Daryl E. Yamaguchi, a principal of the Kahala FRESH brand, recounts the origins of the company, "As a natural food grocer for 20 years, we've learned about the specialty market and developed a commitment to supporting local Hawai'i producers. Our goals include developing a brand that is premium and authentically represents the Hawai'i grown and made image." A product line the company has initially developed focused on targets Japanese visitors, who by tradition purchase *omiyage* when they travel, or high quality edible "souvenirs" for friends and family. Even with their broad experience in retailing, the company reached out to experts at the University of Hawai'i to help develop products for their target markets.

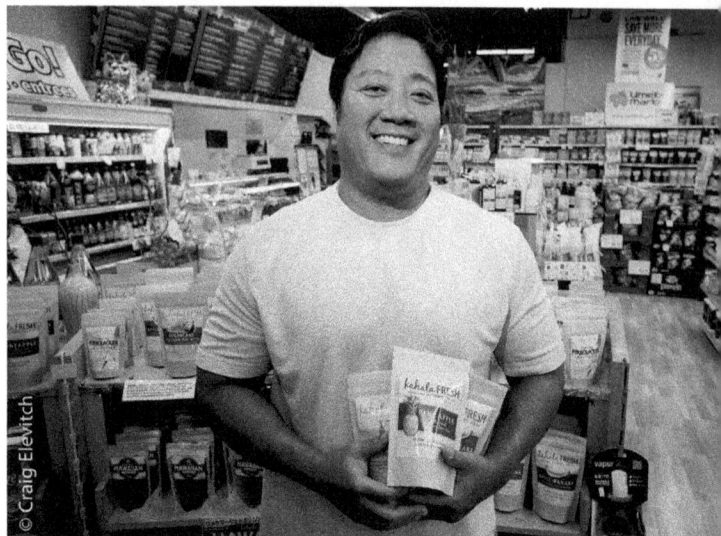

Daryl E. Yamaguchi of Kahala FRESH, with products suited for visitors to take home as high quality edible souvenirs.

Kahala FRESH currently emphasizes quality products made in Hawai'i from local ingredients in portions and packaging suitable for visitors to easily carry home for gifts. The products such as dried apple banana and pineapple are unique and represent the Hawai'i image. "As a business person I understand that due to economics, many companies have to purchase imported ingredients for their products. Our company is different in that we are committed to using Hawai'i-grown ingredients in our products to represent Hawai'i," says Yamaguchi.

Primary markets currently include high-end retailers such as Neiman Marcus and others located in Ward Center and the North Shore of O'ahu. Marketing is done face-to-face with potential customers to communicate the values represented by the brand. Kahala FRESH products were selected for the hospitality bag assembled for delegates of the Asia-Pacific Economic Cooperation (APEC) in November 2011, validating that the brand is reflecting Hawai'i's unique characteristics.

"One of our biggest challenges is to be patient and optimistic that we can grow our products along with the market for local products. Our customers can be proud that they are supporting families of Hawai'i farmers. I am also proud of our production model and all Hawai'i producers that keep a high standard," reflects Yamaguchi regarding living up to the high standards of a Hawai'i-grown and made product line.

Second Skin Naturals™, Moloa'a, Kaua'i

Raven C.J. Liddle, President
www.secondskinnaturals.com

Second Skin Naturals™ produces beauty and skin care products, including its flagship Hawaiian Jungle Shield Spray, salves, scrubs, masks and rejuvenators, all made from certified organic and locally grown ingredients. The company's founder Raven C.J. Liddle created the company out of her personal search for high-quality skin products, finding that the market did not supply what she was seeking. Liddle began researching what ingredients she could grow on her 8-acre farm, while at the same time experimenting with different skin care formulations using extracts of native and introduced species. Currently Liddle grows neem, noni, lemon eucalyptus, kukui, aloe, lemongrass, and many other crops in a certified organic permaculture planting.

Despite the lower cost of imported ingredients, Liddle firmly believes that the ingredients she produces on her farm are superior in quality. "For example, inexpensive aloe juice is readily available from the U.S. mainland. I can extract fresh aloe juice on my farm that contains active enzymes and higher levels of vitamins and minerals than the imported juice—this translates to a much higher quality product that customers prefer. The products are on the shelves within a few days of production," explains Liddle. The products contain naturally occurring plant-derived preservatives, which gives them a 12-month shelf life. In her current sales venues, Liddle estimates that her products are on the shelf for a maximum of 2 months.

Anticipating needing more raw ingredients than she can grow on her farm, Liddle also supplies starter plants to other growers who want to produce ingredients for her. "I am promoting crop and income diversification for other farmers. All the species are selected for high productivity and high price on the market, so that they even have potential to be profitable sold as ingredients," responds Liddle when asked about how other farmers might participate in her farming model. She plans to create a training workbook for farmers about her crops, including spacing, harvesting techniques, and how to grow them in mixed, multistory agroforestry plantings.

"We need to create new crops for commercial farmers. The old crops are fading away," concludes Liddle. Eventually, the plan is to have all of the ingredients used in Second Skin's products be grown by Hawai'i producers and form a growers cooperative alliance.

Second Skin Naturals products are sold in about 150 stores in Hawai'i, online, and through several distributors on the mainland. Currently Liddle does all the marketing herself one-on-one with retailers and distributors. There is no paid advertising—word-of-mouth and personal recommendations are currently sufficient to keep demand rising. Liddle says, "The premium quality of the products translates directly into customer testimonials. Customers think our products are the best of their kind they have ever used." Growth in sales has been 35–40% annually for the past 5 years, according to Liddle.

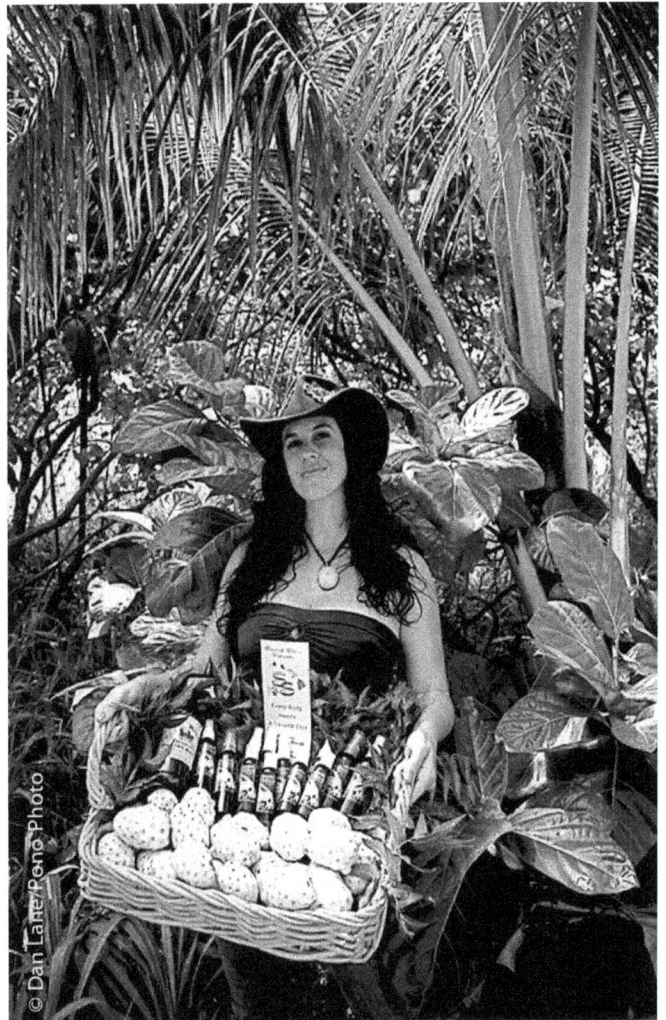

Raven C.J. Liddle of Second Skin Naturals displays some of her skin products made from locally grown, certified organic ingredients.

The company's current challenges include the costs of hiring extra field hands to harvest and process ingredients. This is a secondary motivation to contract with other farmers to produce raw ingredients. Another concern is raising sufficient capital to finance expansion of the company in order to grow at the rate Liddle anticipates.

Liddle has received help from many through the years. First, she has learned from local farmers who have extensive knowledge of soils and growing conditions. Other entrepreneurs have helped guide her by sharing their successes and failures. She has benefitted from indigenous knowledge of different plant species shared by Hawaiian kumu of lāʻau lapaʻau. Finally, "UH's Agricultural Incubator Program and the USDA Farm Services Agency have absolutely supported me and helped me grow," acknowledges a thankful Liddle.

Hawaiian Volcano Sea Salt, Honokaʻa, Hawaiʻi Island

Sam and Paige Wilburn, owners
www.hawaiianvolcanoss.com

Hawaiian Volcano Sea Salt produces naturally smoked Hawaiʻi deep-sea salt. The smoking process takes 24–48 hours using local guava and kiawe (mesquite) wood rather than treating the salt with "liquid smoke," as other companies in Hawaiʻi and elsewhere do. Smoked salt is usually used as finishing salt, sprinkled on dishes just before serving, or used as an ingredient in certain foods and sauces. A byproduct of a deep-sea water desalination plant in North Kona, the salt Hawaiian Volcano Sea Salt uses is much higher in most minerals and 48% lower in sodium than standard commercial table salt.

Trained as architects, owners Sam and Paige Wilburn started their company from scratch out of their own search for a premium smoked salt in Hawaiʻi. They developed their smoking process on a small household grill, sharing batches with friends and family, who eventually encouraged them to start a smoked salt business. Reminiscing about the initial phases of the business, Sam recalls, "My family has several inventors and entrepreneurs and my parents had their own business, which taught me skills in entrepreneurship. My dad Robert and brother Chip

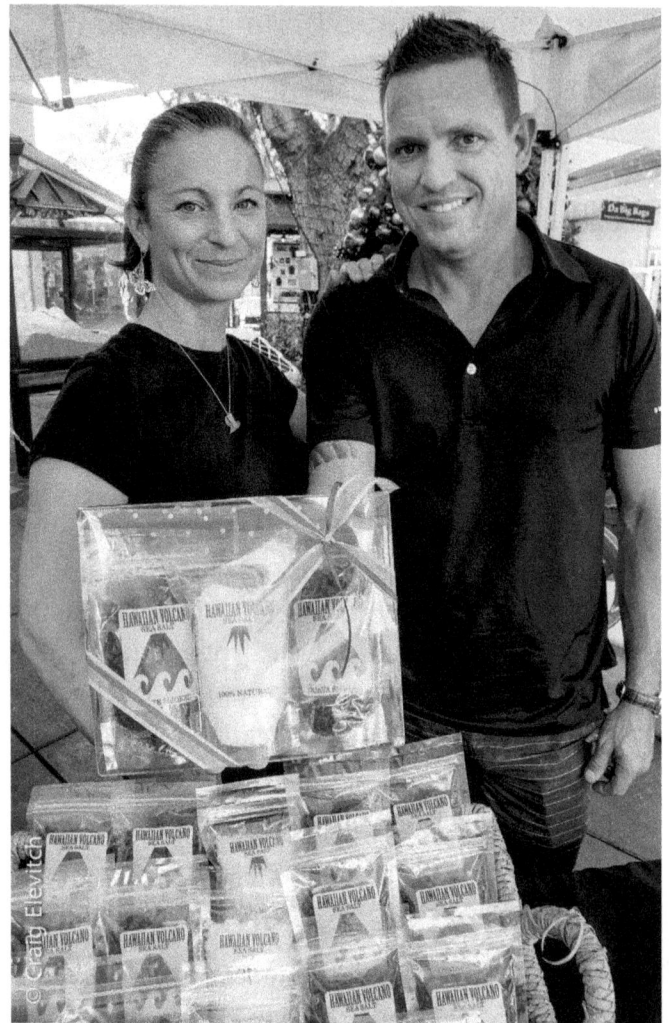

Sam and Paige Wilburn of Hawaiian Volcano Sea Salt display their premium smoked salts at one of the farmers markets where they sell directly to consumers.

helped develop and build the custom smoker we have been using and are currently designing an improved smoker with bigger capacity."

Customer education is a big part of the Wilburn's marketing practice. At $56/lb, their pricing is on par with high quality smoked salts from around the world. Many are not familiar with the use of smoked salts and samples are a key to initiating conversations with potential customers and telling them how the salt is made and used. The company currently sells primarily at farmers markets on Hawaiʻi Island and Oʻahu, which the Wilburns see as perfect venues to interact with customers. The salt is also used by chefs at high-end venues such as Four Seasons Hualālai and the Mauna Lani on the Kohala coast. Imaginative uses such as flavoring ice cream give

Craig Elevitch and Ken Love

chefs a creative incentive to use the salts and provide memorable experiences for their customers.

One of the Wilburns' more successful products is a sampler box containing three of their salts. The sampler makes an easy-to-carry gift for visitors, who later can order their favorites from the company's web site. "We love to educate customers about the unique aroma and flavors of naturally smoked salt," shares Paige. "Our 100% Hawai'i-made product has not only unique flavors of guava and kiawe wood, but we collect our wood from trees growing where they are not wanted, in native forest and in firebreak zones."

One of the challenges this young business faces is the seemingly confusing Hawai'i Department of Health rules regarding production and packaging of smoked salt. As this product is apparently new in Hawai'i, the health inspectors have been unable to give clear guidance about setting up a certified facility for production and packaging. Packaging materials are another challenge, expensive and not readily available in Hawai'i. On the positive side, the Hawai'i Small Business Development Center in Kona has been very helpful with business planning, cash flow budgeting, and product information sheets. Stephanie Donoho of the Big Island Visitors Bureau in Hilo has helped source grant funds, and her husband Paul helped develop the Wilburn's first batch of smoked salt.

Honolulu Gourmet Foods, Honolulu

Jill Lee, Owner
www.honolulugourmetfoods.com

Balancing being a mom and business entrepreneur, Jill Lee built Honolulu Gourmet Foods upon the counter-mainstream model of sourcing locally grown ingredients and making her products exclusively in Hawai'i. "The cost of doing business is high in Hawai'i. At the end of the day, am I proud of my products and our steady customer base confirms that there is a market for high quality, Hawai'i-made products," explains Lee.

Weighing in at fewer than 10 employees, Honolulu Gourmet Foods produces salad dressings, a pesto product line, and a hummus product line (now sold). The company sells its products at a diverse range of markets. Lee has had a booth at KCC Farmers Market for many years and the venue has proven to be

Honolulu Gourmet Foods restaurant at Paradise Palms Café on the University of Hawai'i Mānoa campus, where locally grown prepared food is sold at reasonable prices.

successful on several levels. It allows her to produce in small batches and sell directly to consumers, which is more lucrative than wholesaling. The market has also proven to be an ideal venue for sourcing ingredients directly from farmers. "I've differentiated my product line by utilizing local ingredients and making products in Hawai'i. Partnering with farmers who supply us is essential to our business model. Our suppliers from the KCC Farmers Market have become family," explains Lee. By purchasing directly from farmers, many of Lee's ingredients are less expensive and much higher quality than imported. "Establish long term and friendly relationships with your farmers—you take care of them and they will take care of you. Make life easy for them wherever possible, such as picking up products from a convenient location at a convenient time." To ensure a year-round supply, Lee stockpiles seasonal ingredients, usually by freezing.

The company also sells pesto at Costco, where this product was picked from Lee's line after extensive customer sampling. Once each week, Honolulu Gourmet Foods also sells their locally grown, nutritious meals to employees at Queens and Kaiser Hospital. Additionally, Lee operates a restaurant concession at Paradise Palms Café on the University of Hawai'i Mānoa campus. At this location, students may purchase meals and snacks made from local ingredients purchased directly from farmers and fishermen. "I pitched the idea of serving our food on campus and due to the dearth of local food available for purchase at the university, they loved the idea. Because of the favorable rent agreement, we are able to sell local food at reasonable prices, which is important especially for cash-strapped students," explains Lee proudly. One of Lee's biggest suppliers, the certified organic teaching farm Ma'o Farms in Wai'anae, has many students who attend UH Mānoa and who have access to their own produce even when on campus through Lee's restaurant.

When developing her value-added products, Lee tests small trial batches first, then scales up and re-tests numerous variations until the product is optimized for flavor, aroma, consistency, and a reasonable shelf life. Certain products such as salad dressings require consultation with a food scientist, which Lee has received from people such as Professor Wayne Iwaoka at the UH Mānoa Department of Human Nutrition, Food & Animal Sciences.

Accounting for her success, Lee explains, "My products taste better because they are made from fresh local ingredient in small batches. We make sure our products get sold quickly and do not sit on a shelf for long periods. It would be cheaper to have a mainland company mass-produce products. However, I can tell customers that these are quality ingredients, I know how it was made, and I am proud of it. Customers respond well and so far our unique business model is working."

OnoPops, Hawai'i Kai, O'ahu

Josh Lanthier-Welch and Joe Welch, owners
www.onopops.com

In 2010 brothers Josh Lanthier-Welch and Joe Welch established OnoPops, whose flagship product line consists of ice pops made from local and organic ingredients. Profoundly inspired by the *patela* tradition of ice and milk-based frozen pops in Latin America, the brothers based their product line on a marriage of the Mexican *paleta* and Hawaiian regional cuisine. The result is an endless range of creative flavor combinations that changes continually based on which ingredients are available from local sources. "Chocolate Apple Banana," "Crackseed Lemon Peel," and "Starfruit Lemongrass" are examples of flavors drawn from both the local palate and Hawai'i farms. "Our

OnoPops sources its ingredients almost exclusively from local sources, which differentiates its products from most others in the Hawai'i market.

goal is to get back to local self-sufficiency one pop at time. Eating local can make an amazing treat," says Josh, who is a chef and the culinary expert of the brother team.

OnoPops has differentiated their products by sourcing approximately 95% of their ingredients locally. "We don't just talk the talk—we work tirelessly to source our local ingredients. With very few exceptions, every fruit we use grew in Hawaiian soil," states Josh proudly regarding the core tenet of their business to use local ingredients. The ingredients that they cannot get locally, such as *ume* (Japanese pickled plum) and condensed milk are certified organic, therefore they can state on their web site, "All ingredients are locally sourced, organic, or both." With residents making up about 70% of their customers (30% visitors), the most popular flavors are those based on uniquely local taste preferences such as crack seed, "p to the o to the g" (passion fruit, orange, and guava juices), and mango. In addition to their own culinary expertise, the brothers have gotten insights into incorporating unusual tropical fruits and spices from local experts Maureen and Tane Datta, Ken Love, and the Hawai'i Department of Agriculture web site.

The brothers have developed an imaginative cartoon motif for their labeling and web site. The main flavors each have their own character. The characters live in an imaginary world called Plantation Island where each town on the island represents a different era from Hawai'i's past. The imaginary island and cast of characters strengthens the brand image root-

Craig Elevitch and Ken Love

ed in Hawai'i's agricultural traditions and unique cultural heritage.

Product testing began first with tastings by their families and friends, then rapidly expanding to sales at O'ahu farmers markets, where they still have booths at 6–8 markets per week. Whole Foods and Foodland are currently major retailers, with a range of others including health food stores Kokua Market and Down-to-Earth. A concession at the Punahou School snack bar has also proven to be a profitable sales venue. The company has recently added the UH Mānoa campus, Iolani School, MidPacific Academy, and UH Football at Aloha Stadium as venues, as well as introducing a 4-pack of favorite flavors that is stocked in every Foodland freezer on O'ahu. The company participates in food truck and pop-up events on O'ahu, which allows them to reach different customers than their usual venues. In addition to distributing to O'ahu wholesale and direct-to-consumer markets, OnoPops reaches the other Hawaiian Islands through a major distributor.

One of the major challenges of OnoPops' business is the high price of local ingredients, which they estimate at 3–7 times the cost of imported. There is also the added labor of sourcing local fruits and other ingredients that are not readily available. The company projects that they are close to reaching an economy of scale necessary for profitability and have plans for future expansion into new markets, including their own flagship retail outlet in 2014. Another challenge is competition from new companies who have imitated OnoPops' business model and, in some cases, unique flavor combinations.

Manulele Distillers, LLC, Kunia, O'ahu

Robert Dawson, owner

Start-up company Manulele Distillers specializes in rums distilled from native Hawaiian varieties of sugarcane. After retiring from a career in software development and consulting, owner and founder Robert Dawson went on a life-changing quest for a new business based on Hawai'i-grown crops. He researched the potential for bioenergy crops, but found that they would likely not be feasible without government subsidies. In the course of his bioenergy research, he discovered Hawaiian sugarcane, or

more specifically, the wide range of ancient Hawaiian sugarcane varieties, many of which are still associated with traditional medicine and "love magic." Following a growing fascination, Dawson conceived of a completely vertically integrated business based on growing and processing Hawaiian sugarcane. "Unlike other rums processed in Hawai'i, if we can't grow it here, it won't be in our product. There will be no processed or semi-processed sugar. Only the bottle is imported," states Dawson when describing a core tenet that differentiates his product from others available in Hawai'i. "It's a commitment to local production and part of our branding."

The Hawai'i Agricultural Research Center (HARC) initially provided Dawson with a number of Hawaiian sugarcane varieties, which he cultivated on leased land. In addition to help with his collection from Stefanie Walen (Director of HARC), Noa Lincoln of Amy B.H. Greenwell Ethnobotanical Garden and David Orr of Waimea Valley provided Dawson with additional varieties, increasing the number of varieties he grows to eighteen. After three years growing out his personal collection, Dawson has begun to contract with local farmers to grow cane for him, which greatly expands his production beyond what he is personally able to grow.

Dawson has been building his production facility and retail outlet in Kunia Camp, about 20 minutes northwest of downtown Honolulu. The product line includes white rum, a "cane run" rum with grassy herbal flavor, as well as aged and flavored rums. The facility will also produce sugar syrups for use on pan-

Traditonal Hawaiian sugarcanes are the inspiration for and source of Manulele Distillers' rums and sugar syrups.

cakes, in drinks, etc. Long range plans for the retail outlet include a tasting room, restaurant, and shop for high quality value-added products produced on O'ahu. Anticipating that the local market for his product may becoming a limiting factor, Dawson sees the visitor market as a way to expand. "We want people to experience our products here, then bring them home. We want to serve the local market, but it's limited, so export is the way to grow and expand. Our products are rooted in Hawaiian agriculture and culture, so this is a way to share authentic Hawai'i with the world," reflects Dawson.

Kunia Country Farms, LLC, Kunia, O'ahu

Jason Brand, Cary Takenaka, C. Scott Wo, owners
www.kuniacountryfarms.com

Kunia Country Farms started operations in 2010, transforming former pineapple land in Kunia into a lettuce farm. The farm utilizes an aquaponics system, where crops are grown in containers that float on water. Fish (which are excluded from the crop area) provide a source of fertilizer. "Aquaponics is 6–8 times more productive than ground cropping," estimates co-owner Jason Brand, "which can save costs on land, materials, and labor, allowing us to be competitive with mainland lettuce while delivering a product with a much longer shelf life." The company's growing, harvesting, and packaging operations are continually being refined. "Our number one cost is labor. Mainland producers achieve a cost-effective economy of scale due to large land areas and mechanization. With our relatively small-scale operation, we have to develop other efficiencies in our growing, harvesting, and packaging methods, which we have done."

By late 2012, after expanding twice on borrowed capital, the operation became profitable, with wholesale prices comparable to those of imported mainland sources. Rather than sell at farmers markets, the company has chosen to sell high volumes through wholesale channels. Currently customers include two of the larger supermarkets on O'ahu and several restaurants. Brand projects, "Recent Hawai'i State agricultural statistics show that Hawai'i has been importing 80–85% of lettuce consumed here. We have not yet dented the demand." The company also has a line of gourmet mixed greens for higher end restaurants. Rather than focusing on cutting, washing, and packaging of their mixed greens, they deliver salad mixes still growing in their trays. Restaurants harvest as they use the greens, allowing them to serve the freshest greens possible.

Kunia Country Farms has developed efficient methods of production and harvesting in their aquaponics system that allows them to compete favorably with mainland lettuce in price and quality.

Craig Elevitch and Ken Love

"Our overarching goal is for Hawai'i to become food independent based on sustainable agricultural techniques," articulates Brand when recounting the origins of his business, "and we are doing this by focusing on product niches that are economically feasible in today's marketplace." Although the farm is not certified organic, it is food safety certified, receiving one of the highest certification scores in Hawai'i. Even though food safety certification requires a heavy recordkeeping burden, Brand says, "from a business standpoint I get to see and understand our data. Because we are recording productivity, health of workers, etc., we have important data which we can analyze later on." The owners received food safety training from Jim Hollyer of UH CTAHR's food safety coaching team, including training audits that allowed management to refine and improve their practices. Other technical support for the operation came from aquaponics expert Clyde Tamaru of CTAHR, who assisted by sourcing fish and advising on plant disease issues. Erik Shimizu and Steven Chiang of the Agribusiness Incubator program helped build a cost of production spreadsheet. "These guys really understand the way inputs and outputs work in small businesses," praises Brand.

With an eye towards a bigger goal of Hawai'i food self-sufficiency, Kunia Country Farms supports the local community in several ways: educational tours of their farm upon request, purchasing from other local businesses where possible, and donations to the food bank. "We would like to see a bicycle path through the Kunia area, similar to the Napa Valley bicycle farm tour path. We are looking for ways to support the local economy," envisions Brand.

Pacifikool, Kalihi, O'ahu

Cheryl To, owner
www.pacifikool.com

Cheryl To had been in the restaurant business most of her life when she returned to Hawai'i in 2004 to kick off a new catering business. To quickly recognized that her Island Ginger Ale was a big hit with customers, so by 2006 her catering business transitioned into a drink business based around Hawai'i-grown ginger. The number of flavors has expanded to twelve since then, including "Passionate Ginger,"

Pacifikool's owner Cheryl To created a business beginning with her Island Ginger Ale, expanding to a line of refreshing drinks that evoke "fresh, authentic, Hawai'i' with every sip."

"Liberate a Lime," "Hibiscus Mint Iced Tea," and "Pineapple Ginger," all made primarily from locally grown ginger, fruit, and herbs. To purchases her ginger from farmers on the Hāmākua Coast of Hawai'i Island as well as Thai ginger (*galangal*) from a farmer on O'ahu. To says with pride, "We make our own ginger syrup without preservatives or coloring and, unlike imported bulk commercial ginger, it reproduces the strong, spicy taste of fresh Hawai'i grown ginger. That, and the fact that our ginger is grown in Hawai'i, makes our product totally unique in the marketplace." The company also purchases locally grown mint, spirulina, pineapple juice, lime, lemon, basil, and other ingredients for their made-to-order made drinks. "The only way a product can make it in Hawai'i is to be high-end and not reproducible by imports," reflects To, "and ours exclaim 'fresh, authentic, Hawai'i' with every sip."

Pacifikool's ready-made drinks are available at several farmers markets throughout O'ahu, including the KCC farmers market, a popular venue that To credits with her initial success in the drink business. The company also sells two flavors of ginger syrup, which are sold through a major distributor statewide to hotels, bars, and restaurants. Deliveries are made directly to retail stores. "We participate in the Made in Hawai'i Festival and Hawaii Lodging, Hospitality & Foodservice Expo to get the word out about our products and connect with wholesale customers. Other than those, our advertising is through our web site and by word-of-mouth," explains To regarding her outreach program. "I have learned to listen carefully to customers, and that has gotten us to where we are now."

One of Pacifikool's business challenges has been to raise capital for equipment and expansion. The company was financed from To's savings. "Finding outside investors can be frustrating because it can slow down the process of making expansion decisions," says To. Another challenge is finding reliable labor. "Since we are close to the University of Hawai'i Mānoa campus and KCC, I've been lucky to be able to hire students, some of whom have been our best workers."

To attributes her success to assistance from many quarters, including her whole family's support. She also attributes her success to technical expertise provided by Wayne Inouye of Innovate Hawaii (formerly the Manufacturing Extension Partnership), Joseph Burns of the Hawai'i Small Business Development Center, and Alvin Huang of the Department of Human Nutrition, Food, and Animal Sciences at UH Mānoa. "Participating in the Hawaii Food Manufacturers Association as a board member put me ahead of the game in discovering new opportunities for small businesses in Hawai'i," recounts a thankful To.

Tea Hawaii & Company, Volcano Village, Hawai'i Island

Eva Lee and Chiu Leong, Founders
www.teahawaii.com

Eva Lee and Chiu Leong founded Tea Hawaii & Company with an overarching vision of putting tea front and center as a Hawai'i grown specialty crop. The couple has been growing and processing tea for over ten years and currently engages in all aspects of tea production: growing, processing, marketing, and education. Their products include several 100% Hawai'i-grown single estate whole leaf teas including, "Forest White," "Volcano Green," "Mauka Oolong," and "Makai Black." The first two of these are grown and processed by Lee and Leong and the other two

Freshly brewed Tea Hawaii & Company tea samples at the Waimea Town Market.

were carefully selected to be sold under the Tea Hawaii label (with the source estate clearly identified). The company also processes finished teas for other growers to sell under their own label. Based on their prominent role in promoting Hawai'i grown tea, Lee and Leong provide product development services for other Hawai'i tea farms, including consultation on a customized product line for the specific teas others grow. Additionally, Tea Hawaii propagates tea varieties and sells plants to other farmers and advises on tea horticulture.

In describing her business model, Lee often talks about the big picture, "Spearheading the consciousness of tea requires individual growers that have like minds about community and think beyond self-interest. The private sector needs to join together to develop the industry together. It's a full-time gig to move everything forward." Based on their drive to create a Hawai'i tea industry, Lee and Leong can seem more like extension agents than entrepreneurs at times. The roots of their passion go deep as Lee recounts, "Tea has particular meaning for me, as my father came from the birthplace of tea in China. It was exciting to think of growing a crop with which my family is so connected. Tea culture is also richly intertwined with the arts. As an artist, Chiu has long worked with tea pottery, and we have long been captivated by all of the other experiences that surround tea in the arts: inspired painting, writing, and tea ceremony." All of these connections led to an attrac-

Craig Elevitch and Ken Love

tion to all aspects of tea, which clearly shows in the diversity of Tea Hawaii's activities.

Lee and Leong's tea business came to life in the early 2000s when they heard of research being conducted by Dr. Francis Zee of the USDA Agricultural Research Service in Hilo. Early trials conducted in collaboration with UH College of Tropical Agriculture and Human Resources were promising for production in high elevation areas such as Volcano Village where Lee and Leong live. As the researchers were looking for collaborators in the private sector, the couple saw an opportunity to get involved at an early stage of a potentially important specialty crop for Hawai'i. Eventually they worked closely with Dr. Zee as well as Dwight Sato, Milton Yamasaki, and Dr. C.Y. Hu, University of Hawai'i staff who were involved in the tea project.

In addition to horticultural practices, learning the art of processing finished teas has been central to developing Tea Hawaii's product line. As past project manager for the nonprofit Hawaii Tea Society, Lee brought tea experts from China, Taiwan, and Japan to Hawai'i to teach the art of processing tea. Lee recalls the many years of discovery, "It is fascinating to adapt centuries-old tea expertise from other regions to our conditions. We have gone through a steep learning curve, fusing together very different techniques from various regions to find what can work here. We now know the importance of adapting the processing to our growing and harvest conditions, which is a continual learning process."

Lee and Leong learned industry-standard cupping techniques through the Tea Association USA Specialty Tea Institute certification program, skills that were enriched by visiting experts through the years. "Everyone in the industry needs to learn cupping skills," encourages Lee. "It is essential that we all work together to achieve a high standard for Hawai'i-grown tea. Lee conducts extensive product testing for each new process or new circumstance in her business, including cupping and other sensory evaluations from the time the leaf comes into the workshop. In addition to professional evaluation by tea experts that Tea Hawai'i has consulted with for years, Lee and Leong receive valuable feedback from customers on a weekly basis where they sell their teas at the Waimea Town Market (farmers market). "In order to engage customers, we have to connect with them on a personal level. The farmers market gives us a great opportunity to interact with our customers, where we learn as much or more from them as they do from us."

When asked how Tea Hawaii can compete with less expensive imported teas, Lee responds, "We don't compete—we're not even on the same shelf or shop as imported commodity teas. We make extremely high quality 100% Hawai'i grown teas, or they don't go out on the shelf."

Madre Chocolate, Honolulu

Nat Bletter and David Elliot, Founders
www.madrechocolate.com

With several national and international awards won in 2012, Madre Chocolate has earned its self-ascribed tagline, "Hawai'i's best bean-to-bar chocolate." Cofounder Nat Bletter sums up the company's business philosophy as, "Hawai'i-made chocolate will never be competitive on quantity or price, so our primary focus is on quality and originality." As an ethnobotanist (one who studies the complex relationships between plants and people), Bletter first started making chocolate on a dare from a friend to put his academic knowledge into practice. His initial experiments were enthusiastically received by friends, family and colleagues, inspiring him to continue professionally. Now Nat's official title is "Chocolate Flavormeister"

Cofounders Nat Bletter (left) and David Elliot (right) demonstrate the art of chocolate making in one of their classes.

for the company, with cofounder David Elliot taking on the role of production manager. Both Bletter and Elliot had long experience in Mexico and Central America before putting down roots in Hawai'i. This bicultural context explains the company's two distinct lines of bar chocolate, "Xocolatl," incorporating Mexican flavors and inspired by traditional chocolates of Central and South America, and "Kokoleka," made from Hawai'i grown cacao and incorporating a distinctly Hawaiian flavor palette. In addition to these two regular lines, the company makes limited edition flavors, as ingredient availability and creative whim allow.

A challenge faced by the company in developing its Hawai'i locavore Kokoleka line was to find sources for high quality cacao in Hawai'i. According to Bletter, Hawaiian cacao is 3–5 times more expensive than the best cacao in the world, therefore quality is of paramount importance, beginning with how the cacao is cultivated. The company works closely with its farmers, as Bletter notes, "We purchase directly from farmers in Hawai'i, allowing us to offer suggestions on their growing, harvesting, and postharvest practices. We visit our farmers twice a month so that we can have a continuing dialog about how cultivation practices affect the end product and how to bring out specific flavors we are looking for." Madre Chocolate's farmers are also in charge of the critical fermentation process, which is carried out shortly after harvest. Because fermentation greatly affects the flavor profile of the chocolate, Bletter works with farmers to develop their process. "Hawai'i is in the northern most range of cacao, with temperatures that are often a bit cool for proper fermentation. Getting fermentation right is the hardest part of chocolate here and it requires experience and skill to get it right. However, having our farmers take care of the fermentation for us adds value to their product

and it is part of our mission to compensate farmers as much as possible," says Bletter. The company has worked closely with other experts on developing their fermentation, including University of Hawai'i's chocofiles H.C. "Skip" Bittenbender and Daniel O'Doherty.

Madre Chocolate has a range of sales venues, beginning with its own retail shop in Kailua, O'ahu. The company distributes wholesale to 30–40 retail stores in Hawai'i, as well as to retailers in most major cities on the U.S. mainland, Sweden, Germany, the Netherlands, and Belgium. Their products are sold through their booths at 3–4 farmers markets per week on O'ahu. Additionally, all products are available through their web site. With the limited supply of Hawaiian cacao, a small-scale production facility, and international recognition, it is no surprise that Madre is currently "selling every chocolate bar a few weeks before making it," according to Bletter.

Educational classes and agritourism have become another popular aspect of the business. Bletter and Elliot began by presenting bean-to-bar chocolate classes, then added truffle making, and now also conduct regular cacao farm and chocolate factory tours. When asked if the potential for training new competitors through classes and tours is a concern, Bletter responds, "When we educate people about artisan chocolate, we create more customers. Our purpose is to build a bigger pie, rather than a bigger piece of a smaller pie." Bletter also sees agritourism as crucial for the Hawai'i chocolate business, "Hawai'i is the only place in the U.S. where cacao grows, so we have the unique opportunity to show people not just bean to bar, but tree to bar. This makes us unique in the world, as even in other chocolate growing regions, there are only a handful of places where people can experience chocolate from the field to finished products."

Craig Elevitch and Ken Love

EXAMPLE CROPS

The following crops illustrate important concepts in adding value. The purpose is not to promote these specific crops so much as to illustrate value-added concepts that are widely applicable. For these crops, as for all crops, the cost of production should be calculated and weighed against estimated market prices before investing in production. Cost of production spreadsheets for many crops are available at the UH Mānoa College of Tropical Agriculture and Human Resources (CTAHR) web site (www.ctahr.hawaii.edu/Site/Info.aspx).

Avocado

Evaluating local premium varieties

(adapted from Elevitch and Love 2011)

Avocados must have to come to Hawai'i with the first traders. It is estimated that there are currently well over 200 named types in Hawai'i, with wide variation in taste and other qualities. This genetic diversity is a basis for development of specialty varieties with outstanding qualities.

Products and markets

Avocado fruit is consumed in various ways around the world. In the U.S., it is commonly used in salads and sandwiches. Guacamole, a Mexican dish made with avocado, lemon, and spices, is also very popular.

The large number of named types in Hawai'i hints at the potential for developing specialty avocado varieties with outstanding qualities. (variety poster © Love 2009, www.hawaiifruit.net/indexposter.html)

Some eat avocado sweetened with sugar. In Brazil, avocado is commonly added to ice cream and milk shakes. Oil expelled from the flesh is used in cooking, salad dressings and as a constituent in cosmetics. Several parts of the plant are used in folk medicine.

Avocados are commonly available wherever produce is sold. In Hawai'i, unique as well as commercially selected varieties are available at farmers markets and food retailers.

As with all fruit, offering perfect, unblemished fruit is essential for reaching the highest value markets. Selling varieties with unique characteristics such as nutty, rich flesh will attract higher prices. Locally developed varieties can have an advantage in the marketplace, especially for those who prefer to buy locally grown produce even when they are more familiar with imported varieties such as Haas. Locals in Hawai'i often ask for "butter pears," high oil content Hawai'i varieties such as Yamagata, Kahalu'u and Malama. Organic certification may give an advantage in certain markets, such as health food stores, but this advantage may not translate into higher prices. High-quality off-season varieties may also fetch higher prices.

Multiple cropping systems

The tree casts a dense shade, so its use is limited as an overstory species to shade-tolerant crops. Even so, scattered avocado trees are commonly found in coffee orchards in Kona, Hawai'i. Producing fruit for home use or sales outweighs the reduction in area for coffee cultivation. Avocado makes an acceptable component in a multi-row windbreak, although some wind damage to fruit can be expected.

Description

Avocado trees can reach 18 m (60 ft) or more in height, but trees are pruned to keep them about 3.5 m (12 ft) for ease of harvesting. Avocado is the only important fruit in the laurel family (Lauraceae). There are three races, West Indian, Mexican, and Guatemalan, each with distinct fruit characteristics. Commercial varieties have been selected from each of these three races, as well as from hybrids between them. Most marketed fruit come from the hundreds of natural occurring hybrids growing throughout Hawai'i.

Environment

Each race has different environmental tolerances, with the West Indian race more tropical (heat tolerant and cold sensitive) and the Mexican and Guatemalan races are more subtropical (more heat sensitive and cold tolerant). The tree requires well drained soils—waterlogging for more than a day can be fatal. Although drought tolerant, continual soil moisture is required for good fruit production. Fruit set is poor in extended wet periods, due to anthracnose.

Bilimbi

Adapting a savory Southeast Asian fruit

(adapted from Love and Paull 2011a)

Bilimbi is closely related to starfruit (*Averrhoa carambola*). It originated in Southeast Asia and is claimed as a native by Malaysia and the Indonesian Moluccas. The fruit was taken from Timor to Jamaica in 1793, supposedly in Captain William Bligh's second breadfruit voyage, and was distributed widely in the New World. It may have to come to Hawai'i with the first immigrants from the Philippines in 1906. In 1815, "almost sweet" forms of the fruit were first found in the Philippines, but sour forms were preferred. Some of these almost-sweet forms are still found in the Philippines but are not known to be present in Hawai'i. The tree is cultivated throughout Indonesia, Malaysia, the Philippines, India, and Sri Lanka on a small scale and is frequently found as a backyard tree. It is also common in other Southeast and South Asian countries and is now found worldwide.

Products and markets

Bilimbi fruit is too acid to be eaten fresh and commonly is used for pickles, curries, chutney, and preserves. It is also made into a cooling drink similar to lemonade. In the Philippines the fruit is used as the basis of soup stock and in stews. In Hawai'i, chefs use juiced fruit as a substitute for vinegar in salad dressings and soups. It is also dried and reconstituted with other juices and spices for use in sauces. The sour taste of bilimbi is due to its high oxalic acid content, which ranges from 10.5 to 14.7 mg/g in green fruit and from 8.45 to 10.8 mg/g in ripe fruit. The fruit can be used to remove rust stains and to clean knife blades. There are many uses in traditional medicine.

Craig Elevitch and Ken Love

Description

Bilimbi can reach 15 m (50 ft) in height but is usually kept shorter to facilitate harvesting. Heavy pruning can suppress flowering. The tree forms 18–64 flowers in panicles on the trunk and older branches. The waxy, pale green fruit is slightly lobed, about 10 cm (4 in) long and up to 2.5 cm (1 in) wide. The sour fruit changes from green to light yellow when ripe. It matures 50–60 days after flowering. The tree is tropical and extremely sensitive to cold and wind.

Environment

Depending on rain or the frequency of irrigation, the tree can fruit multiple times a year in Hawai'i. At other times it fruits once or twice a year for a period of 2 months. The trees thrive in full sun and will grow in most types of soil. The tree has been observed in Hawai'i up to 1070 m (3500 ft) elevation. Another tree at 90 m (300 ft) elevation at a South Kona test plot produced fruit year-round with irrigation.

Breadfruit

A traditional Hawaiian starch with import replacement potential

(adapted from Ragone 2011)

The wild, seeded, ancestor of breadfruit, *Artocarpus camansi*, or breadnut, is native to New Guinea, and possibly the Moluccas (Indonesia) and the Philippines. Breadfruit, both seeded and seedless forms, does not naturally occur in the Pacific Islands. This species was first domesticated in the western Pacific and spread by humans throughout the region beginning 3,000 or more years ago. Breadfruit is found throughout the tropics and cultivated on most Pacific islands.

Products and markets

Breadfruit produces abundant, nutritious fruit (i.e., high in carbohydrates and a good source of fiber, vitamins, and minerals) that is typically cooked and consumed as a starchy staple when firm and mature. Mature fruit can be processed into fries, chips and other snacks, dips or spreads, "veggie" burgers, beverages, dried into flour, and minimally processed or frozen. Breadfruit flour can be partially substituted for wheat flour in many bread, pastry, pasta, and

Bilimbi has potential for use in pickles, curries, chutney, and preserves.

Pastes and poultices of the leaves are used for coughs, itches, skin swellings, and rheumatism, and fruit conserves or syrups are also used for coughs, fevers, and inflammation.

The sour bilimbi has yet to become popular with a large number of consumers, and grocery store sales are very limited in most Hawai'i markets. The grocery stores that offer bilimbi either sell the fruit in bulk or in small plastic "clamshells." The chefs that utilize bilimbi order 5-pound clamshell packages. The fruit sells from $2.00 to 3.50 a pound. At farmers markets fruit can found in bulk or in small clamshell containers and usually sell for 25¢ each or five for $1.00. Having recipes from chefs available at a Kona farmers' market helped to increase sales to customers unfamiliar with bilimbi. Juiced and dried fruit can be frozen or preserved for future use.

snack products. Ripe, sweet fruit can be eaten raw or cooked and used in pastries, desserts, beverages, and other products. Seeds, cooked in the fruit and eaten throughout the Pacific Islands—but rarely in Polynesia—are high in protein, relatively low in fat and a good source of vitamins and minerals. Breadnut seeds tend to be larger and sweeter than breadfruit seeds and can be roasted or boiled. Cooked seeds be processed into dips, spreads, or pâté. In Ghana, breadfruit and breadnut seeds have been made into nutritious baby food. In the Philippines, immature fruit is sliced, cooked, and eaten as a vegetable.

Breadfruit is a cultural icon in the Pacific. All parts are used medicinally, especially the latex, leaf tips, and inner bark. The wood is lightweight, flexible, and may resist termites. It is used for buildings and canoes. The attractive wood is easily carved into statues, bowls, and other objects. Older, less productive trees are utilized as firewood throughout the region. The inner bark is used to make bark cloth (*kapa* or *tapa*), but this formerly widespread custom is now only practiced in the Marquesas and recently has been revitalized in Hawai‘i. Large, flexible leaves are used to wrap foods for cooking in earth ovens. The sticky white latex is used as a chewing gum and adhesive and was formerly widely used to caulk canoes and as birdlime (to catch birds). Dried male flowers can be burned to repel mosquitoes and other flying insects.

Development of products for import replacement is the most cost effective and beneficial to the local economy. The simplest, most cost- and energy-efficient means of processing breadfruit is to slice or shred raw fruit, dry the pieces using a solar dryer/dehydrator (electric dryers are more energy intensive), and grind into a coarse meal or flour. Breadfruit flour is gluten free can be used as a partial substitute for imported wheat flour in breads, cakes, pastas, crackers, and pastries, and is suitable for export. Ground meal from the otherwise waste skins and cores can be used as a component of animal feed.

Ripe fruit can be dried in thin sheets as a delicious "fruit leather" or mixed with other locally grown products to create fruit bars. Chips and other snack foods fried in coconut or other oil, can be sold locally. For export, these snacks require greater investment in energy, equipment, packaging materials, and preservatives to maintain freshness and quality.

There are several promising specialty markets, including

- Organic and natural foods
- Gluten free
- Traditional Pacific Island diets

The historical importance of breadfruit and name recognition in many countries (based on its connection to *Mutiny on the Bounty*) could play a key factor in marketing. Specialty varieties identified by region could also be helpful in reaching unique markets.

Multiple cropping systems

Breadfruit trees provide shade, mulch, and a beneficial microclimate. They are generally included in home gardens or mixed agroforestry systems with other useful plants. Widely spaced trees (12 m × 12 m [40 ft × 40 ft] are recommended for commercial production) in an orchard can be interplanted with small fruit trees and a leguminous cover crop. Short-term fruit crops (e.g., pineapple, banana, and papaya) or field and vegetable crops (e.g., taro, tomato, and eggplant) can also be grown between young breadfruit trees. A leguminous cover crop should replace these intercrops when they begin to interfere with orchard operations.

Description

Breadfruit is an attractive evergreen tree, typically 12–15 m (40–50 ft) tall with a 0.3–1 m (1–3.2 ft) di-

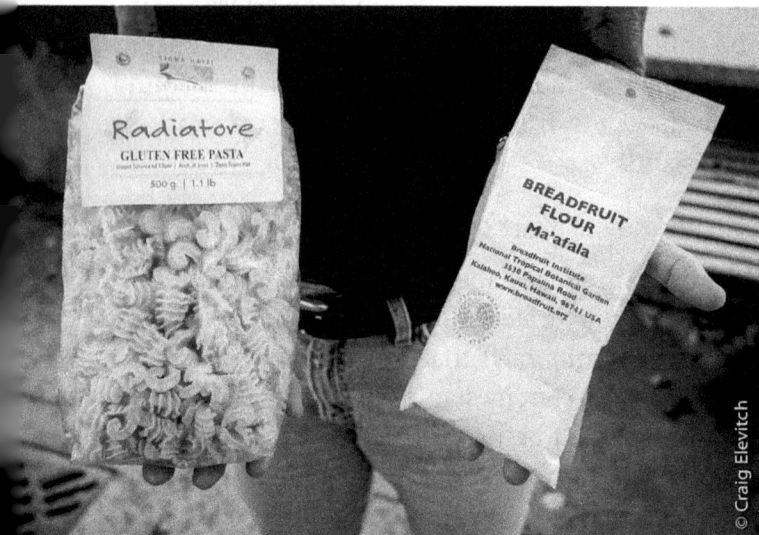

Flour is one of the many shelf-stable processed products that can be made from breadfruit.

Craig Elevitch and Ken Love

ameter trunk, often with buttress roots. Trees can readily be pruned to make it easier to reach and harvest the fruit.

Citrus

New life for locally superior varieties

(adapted from Elevitch and Love 2011)

All *Citrus* species are important for their fruit, which is eaten fresh or processed in numerous ways in cooked dishes, sauces, and beverages. The fruit is preserved in many forms including marmalade, jam, or candied. The pulp and other by-products from juice production are used as cattle feed. An industrial extract of grapefruit seeds and pulp is used to produce a potent topical anti-bacterial and fungicidal agent. Citrus is one of the most important honeybee forage plants in many parts of the world. Oils in the peel, leaf, and flower are used in cosmetics and as medicinals. Citrus species are important in traditional Pacific Island medicine.

With numerous species and varieties of citrus planted throughout the Pacific, there are many opportunities to develop locally superior varieties. A good example is the orange-fleshed Rangpur lime, which became naturalized in Kona, Hawai'i, and developed into a new recognized variety called Rangpur Kona Lime (*Citrus × limonia* Osbeck). With a unique flavor profile and unusual orange color, Kona lime is an excellent example of a specialty crop developed from a locally adapted variety. Building a regional identity for a unique variety such as Kona lime can add val-

ue by increasing recognition and therefore demand. Knowing the stories behind the different citrus types and varieties will help increase sales at farmers markets. For example, people appreciate the story of how pummelo was used by the Chinese as currency when trading with India in the 1400s. Proper tree pruning can increase percentage of perfect fruit. Most citrus can be stored at 2–4°C (36–39°F) for up to 5 months.

Markets for fresh fruit are found in all sectors. For unique varieties, farmers markets and restaurants may be the most lucrative. For example, the specialty market for Kona lime has recently been developed in Kona, Hawai'i among chefs. Citrus preserves are commonly found in farmers markets, grocery stores and in gift shops. Citrus trees loaded with brightly colored fruit are an essential component of agtourism including "you pick" destinations.

Multiple cropping systems

Citrus trees can be grown together with shade-tolerant crops such as coffee and vanilla with appropriate spacing to avoid over-shading. Citrus trees are very common in mixed perennial gardens around homes, where three to four species are often found for fruit, juice, flavorings, and as ornamentals. Thorny types may be useful for living fences, especially when trimmed into dense hedges.

Description

Citrus are shrubs to medium-size trees up to about 6 m (20 ft) in height, although some species can reach 15 m (50 ft). Rootstocks can greatly affect the height of grafted trees. Trees have thin, smooth, and gray-brown to greenish bark. Most species are single-trunked with very hard wood. Canopy widths range from slender to broad, depending on species. Many cultivated species are pruned so that the canopy is as wide as the tree is tall.

Environment

Suitable climates for citrus are the tropical and subtropical humid regions. In the subtropics, citrus grows between sea level and 750 m (2450 ft) above sea level. In the tropics, citrus does well below 1600 m (5250 ft). Mean annual rainfall is 900–3000 mm (35–120 in). Without irrigation, 900 mm (35 in) per annum is typically needed for any significant

Citrus species commonly found in Hawai'i

Species	Common name	Size and spines
C. aurantifolia	lime	shrub/small tree to 4 m (13 ft), spiny
C. aurantium	sour orange	tree to 10 m (33 ft), short spines
C. grandis	pummelo	tree to 12 m (40 ft), spiny
C. hystrix	Kaffir lime	tree to 5 m (16 ft), short spines
C. limon	lemon	tree to 6 m (20 ft), stout spines
C. macroptera	wild orange	tree to 5 m (16 ft), spiny
C. medica	citron	shrub to 3 m (10 ft)
C. mitis	calamondin	tree to 12 m (40 ft), spiny
C. paradisi	grapefruit	tree to 15 m (50 ft)
C. reticulata	mandarin	tree to 9 m (30 ft), usually spiny
C. sinensis	sweet orange	tree to 12 m (40 ft), often spiny

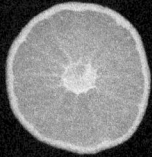

BIG ISLAND CITRUS

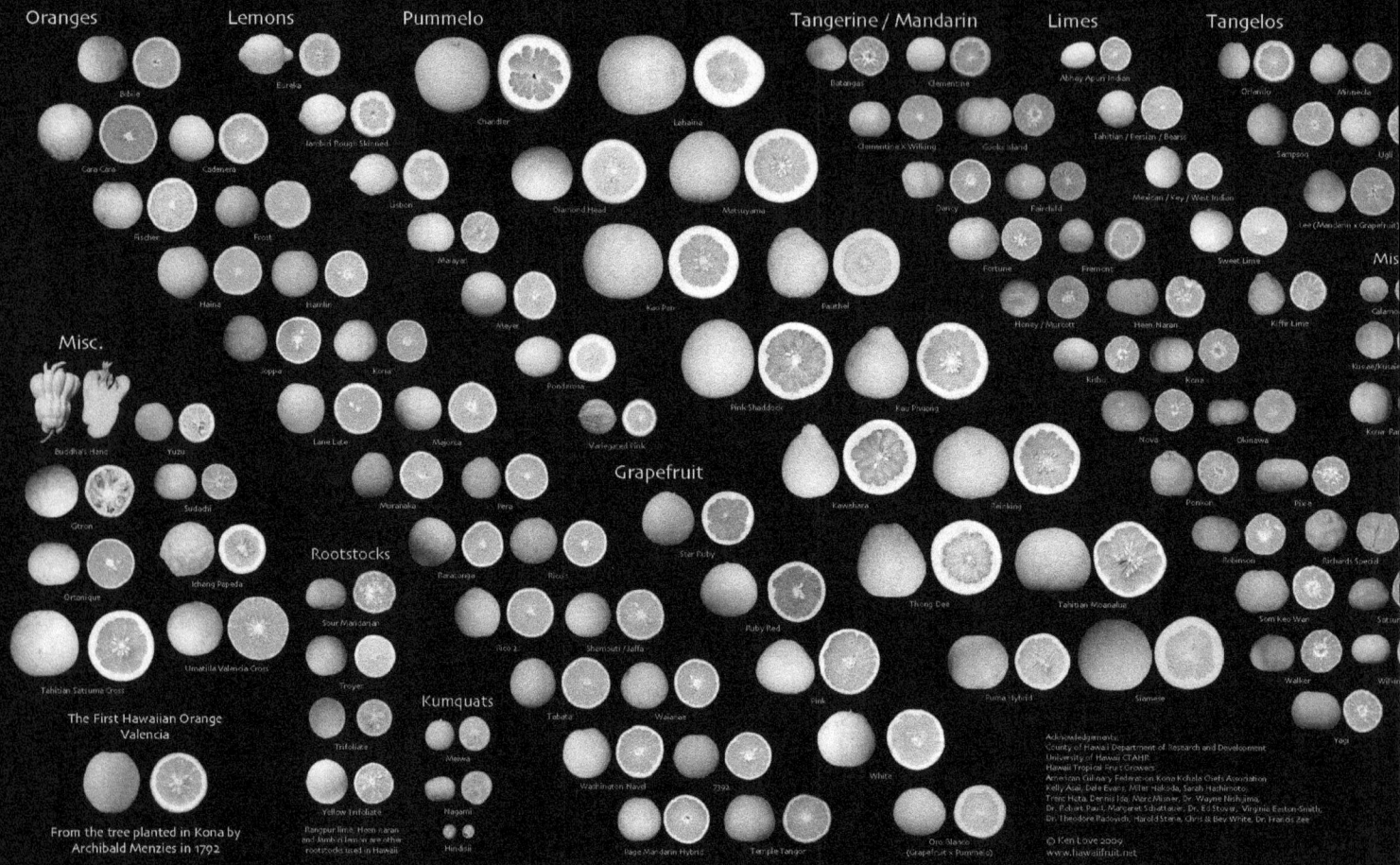

Citrus varieties that have been selected locally or that are unusual in the marketplace, offer good potential for profitable products. (variety poster © Love 2009, www.hawaiifruit.net/indexposter.html)

fruit production. Optimum daytime temperatures are 25–30°C (77–86°F), but temperatures can reach 43°C (110°F) in Southern California and other citrus-growing regions. Citrus tolerates a wide range of soils, from almost pure sands to organic mucks to heavy clay soils. The trees do not stand waterlogged soils but grow well in freely draining soils.

Fig

Variety trials for Hawai'i environments

(adapted from Elevitch and Love 2011)

Believed to be indigenous to Asia Minor, the fig spread beyond the Mediterranean region before recorded history. Hiram Bingham first reported the fig in Hawai'i in 1825. There are about 1,000 varieties of figs worldwide, which are usually described by their size, fruit color, and leaf shape. The most common

types found in Hawai'i are Brown Turkey and White Kadota. Currently, field trials are underway to select additional varieties with unique color, flavor, and texture in Hawai'i. The best of these varieties will become high-value specialty figs for the local market.

Products and markets

Figs are generally consumed fresh, peeled or unpeeled. Fresh fruit is also used in many cooked dishes such as cakes and pies, pudding, and bread. Figs are also preserved in various ways such as dehydration, jam, and as whole fruits in syrup. Off-grade figs have been roasted and used as a coffee substitute or fermented to produce alcohol. Figs are high in fiber with several purported beneficial effects such as lowering blood pressure, controlling cholesterol, imparting a feeling of fullness, which can be useful for weight-loss diets. Figs are a good source of po-

Craig Elevitch and Ken Love

tassium and vitamin B$_6$. Fruit, leaves, and latex have been used in various folk remedies in Latin America.

Figs lend themselves to a wide variety of value added products. Unblemished and optimally ripened figs have the highest value. This requires regular picking, preferably daily. Figs are fragile and should be placed in containers at the time of harvest so that they do not press on each other. Latex oozing from the stem end should not be allowed to contact the fruit skin, as it will cause discoloration. Fully ripe figs are very perishable and should be chilled as soon as possible after harvest to −1–0°C (30–32°F) at 90–95% relative humidity for storage up to 30 days. Protection from birds by bagging fruit or netting trees is essential to ensure unblemished fruit. Fruit fly traps may aid in reducing fruit fly damage where problematic.

Current field trials will eventually lead to selections of high-quality fig varieties for Hawaiian environments and markets. (variety poster © Love 2007, www.hawaiifruit.net/indexposter. html)

Matching variety to elevation and other environmental conditions is important to ensure reliable and high yields, in addition to fruit quality.

The most promising market in Hawai'i is for fresh fruit sold in farmers markets, grocery stores, and restaurants. The most lucrative markets for newly introduced varieties with exceptional color and taste may be in the visitor industry, i.e., hotel restaurants and visitor gift boxes. Catering to chefs is a potential niche market, as they often have special requests (such as for 80% ripe fruit), which can be filled as a custom product.

Description

In Hawai'i the tree grows rapidly and can achieve heights of 9 m (30 ft) or more. Figs should be pruned to keep low (less than 2 m [7 ft]) to facilitate harvesting. Fruit generally only forms on new growth. In many growing regions, figs are pruned severely after harvest to stimulate new growth for fruit production. Fig belongs to the Moraceae family, which includes breadfruit (*Artocarpus altilis*), jackfruit (*Artocarpus heterophyllus*), and mulberry (*Morus* spp.).

Environment

Some types of figs are cultivated from sea level to over 1,500 m (5,000 ft) and can be grown in many microclimates. The trees can grow in most soils with good drainage. They are tolerant of some salinity but do not like highly acidic soils. Figs are drought tolerant.

Jackfruit

A fruit with hundreds of potential value-added products

(adapted from Love and Paull 2011b and Elevitch and Manner 2006)

Jackfruit is thought to have originated in southwest India and been spread in ancient times throughout Southeast Asia, then to tropical Africa. It was probably introduced to the Philippines in the 12th century and domesticated soon thereafter. The writings of Pliny the Elder, as early as AD 100, mention jackfruit's origin as "where the Indian sages and philosophers do ordinarily live." The tree is still highly regarded by subsistence farmers from India to South-

Adding Value to Locally Grown Crops in Hawai'i

Dried jackfruit ("jerky") and marmalade, two of the hundreds of processed products that can be made from jackfruit.

east Asia for its fruit, timber, and medicinal uses. It was one of the earliest cultivated fruits. Jackfruit was reported in Hawai'i prior to 1888.

Products and markets

Hundreds of value-added products can be made from jackfruit seeds as well as ripe and half-ripe pulp. In India and other parts of Asia and the South Pacific, the half-ripe fruit is commonly cooked into curries, soups, and stews. It can be pickled, dried, and canned. Vacuum dried jackfruit chips are sold widely in Southeast Asia in sealed bags as a snack. It is also used as flavoring for ice cream or made into pudding, gum, and beverages. The seeds are usually boiled and eaten as a snack, although in South India they are often dried and milled into flour used for *dosa* or confections. This gluten-free seed flour can serve as a substitute for wheat for those with specific food allergies. Leaves are used for cooking and wrapping foods, and the wood is used for utensils, fencing, fodder, and fuel.

Whole jackfruit in Hawai'i is usually sold by size. At some markets it might be sliced into sections and sold in bags; state health officials frown upon this practice unless the fruit was cut in a certified kitchen and kept chilled at the market. Some Hawai'i wholesalers will pay from $1.50 to $2.00 a pound for the fruit, but sales are infrequent and dependant on chefs' needs. At some farmers markets, dried jackfruit retails for an average of $5.00 for a 2 oz bag. Seeds are seldom sold in Hawai'i but are sometimes given out

as samples at farmers markets. Chefs in Hawai'i are just beginning to work with jackfruit, and demand for the fruit is expected to increase.

Multiple cropping systems

During the early years, jackfruit can be successfully intercropped with a number of short-term crops such as legumes, vegetables, and banana. The intercrop makes use of the unproductive space available in the early years and gives an income before the jackfruit trees come into production. As the trees grow closer, the crops grown among the trees can be replaced by a permanent ground cover. Perennial crops such as durian, coffee, and citrus can be grown together with jackfruit, given wider spacing between jackfruit trees to allow sufficient space for the other crop trees.

Description

The evergreen, latex-producing jackfruit tree can reach up to 24 m (80 ft) in height, with a straight stem that branches near the base. The tree produces a long taproot. All parts have milky white, very sticky latex. The jackfruit flowers are borne on short shoots on the trunk and older branches. The thick, rubbery rind has short, blunt spines, and the fruit can have up to 500 seeds. Average fruit size is about 16 kg (35 lb), but they are often much larger. In 2010, at a jackfruit festival in Kerala, India, a 65 kg (144 lb) fruit was featured. The largest Hawaiian fruit was 36 kg (79 lb) and held the Guinness book of records for a number of years. In locations where the fruit is relished, only the rind and core are not consumed.

Environment

Jackfruit thrives in tropical warm and humid frost-free climates at elevations below 1525 m (5000 ft). The trees have some salinity tolerance but poor drought and flooding tolerance. It will grow in a variety of well-drained soils with a pH between 5 and 7.5. The tree does not do well in exposed locations with strong, drying winds. It needs irrigation in times of drought in order to produce fruit. Growth habits vary from tall and straight with a thin trunk to short with a thick trunk, varying with soil type, environment, and cultivar.

Craig Elevitch and Ken Love

'Ōhelo berry

Native plant domestication and variety selection

(adapted from Elevitch and Love 2011)

'Ōhelo berry, native only to Hawai'i, has not been domesticated until recently. A project undertaken by the USDA has developed types both for berry production and for ornamental use. As a native plant, 'ōhelo berry has unique appeal to chefs and others who are always looking for specialty ingredients with a Hawaiian character.

Products and markets

'Ōhelo berry is a small native Hawaiian shrub related to cranberry and blueberry. It is endemic to Hawai'i, i.e., found nowhere else in the world. The cranberry-like fruit is used primarily to make jam and jelly, but is also used in various dishes and baked goods. New markets for 'ōhelo as an indigenous ornamental plant are also being developed.

'Ōhelo berry is usually processed into jam or jelly and sold in farmers markets and grocery stores throughout Hawai'i. One market is higher-end restaurants who aspire to diversify their offerings by incorporating uniquely Hawaiian ingredients. The fruit is used both as a sweet and a savory in these dishes.

'Ōhelo is also sold unprocessed to hotel chefs and jelly makers. A wide range of products incorporating this fruit can be envisaged: sauces, flavorings, and fruit mixes. Its status as the only endemic Hawaiian fruit that is commercially used imparts a unique identity, which adds significantly to its value compared with similar exotic fruits.

Multiple cropping systems

Because 'ōhelo berry has only recently been brought into cultivation, there are no examples of integrating the plant in agroforestry systems. However, due to its natural tendency to colonize disturbed or exposed drier lava sites, it has potential to be grown as an understory crop in an open orchard on such sites.

Description

The small shrub reaches 10–130 cm (4–50 in) in height. Berries vary widely in color from yellow to red to dull black.

Environment

'Ōhelo berry is commonly found at elevations of 640–3,700 m (2,100–12,000 ft) on Maui and Hawai'i islands, but also grows on Kaua'i, O'ahu, and Moloka'i. It usually grows as a pioneer on exposed lava flows, such as alpine or subalpine shrubland. When in season, Hawai'i residents gather 'ōhelo berries from the National Parks and high elevations to process into jam, jelly and pie filling. Potential negative impacts of wild gathering activities may include spreading of invasive weed species, and competing for berries with the endemic nene goose.

Left: Beautiful flowers of 'ōhelo berry. Middle: 'Ōhelo berry shrub with ripe fruit. Right: The beautiful foliage of 'ōhelo berry lends itself to growing this plant both for fruit and ornamental purposes.

Rollinia

Introducing a new tropical fruit

(adapted from Love and Paull 2011c and Elevitch and Love 2011)

Thought to have originated in Northern Brazil along the banks of the Amazon, rollinia is now found growing in all tropical locations and rapidly becoming a favorite with tropical fruit aficionados. By introducing this unusual looking fruit to consumers, it has good potential to become a popular specialty fruit in new markets.

Products and markets

The fruit, often described as having a caramel, lemon custard pudding flavor, is usually eaten out of hand. Rollinia fruit can also be made into sauces, ice cream, flan and other desserts. It is often juiced in Brazil and sometimes blended with milk for a drink. It has also been made into wine. The wood is hard and used in canoes, boat masts, and other durable uses.

Commercial fruit is generally harvested mature and beginning to ripen, when it starts to soften and turn yellow. Care in handling is highly recommended, as the fruit protuberances and skin will blacken considerably when touched.

Farmers markets and health food stores are primary markets. This fruit is rapidly gaining favor with chefs and larger groceries featuring locally grown produce for the adventurous consumer.

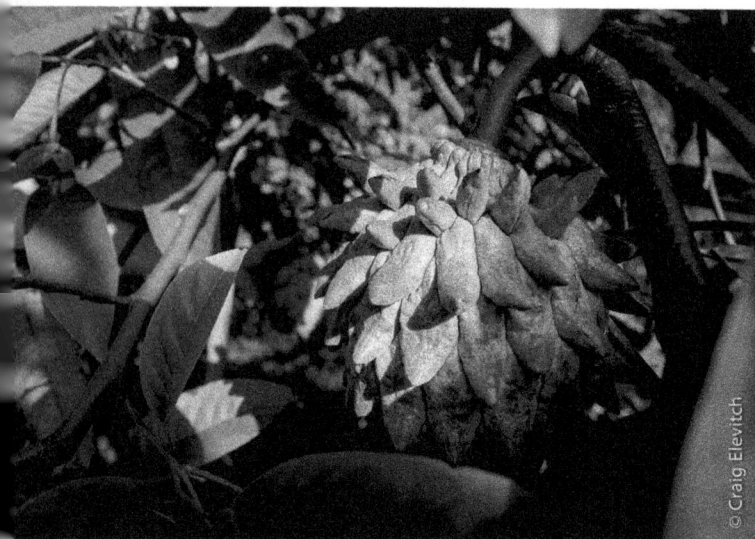

The unusual looking rollinia fruit has flesh that tastes like caramel lemon custard. The fruit has good potential as a new commercial crop in Hawai'i.

Multiple cropping systems

In favorable environments, rollinia grows quickly and can bear fruit within 2–3 years of planting from seed or grafting. This makes it a good candidate for early yields in a multispecies planting with other fruits and nuts that take longer to begin production. Appropriately pruned to maintain canopy size (and facilitate ease of harvesting), the tree can make a good companion to shade-tolerant understory crops.

Description

The fast growing tropical tree can reach heights of 15 m (50 ft). The fruit is highly inconsistent in shape and size. It turns from green to yellow when ripe. The milky white flesh usually contains black seeds averaging a 1.2 cm (0.5 in) in length. Some seedlings will produce fruit in 2–3 years while others will produce in 5–6 years. In many parts of Hawai'i, fruiting occurs year round when rainfall is abundant. Rollinia is in the Annonaceae family, which includes other popular fruits such as cherimoya, sugar apple, and soursop.

Environment

Rollinia prefers hot, humid climates. The tree thrives where rainfall is evenly distributed throughout the year. It does not tolerate cold or extended drought. It prefers deep, rich, well drained organic soil and benefits from copious amounts of mulch. Rollinia tolerates poorer and highly acidic soils as long as there is sufficient water. In Hawai'i, trees can be found from sea level to 900 m (3,000 ft).

Surinam cherry

Chef-driven demand

(adapted from Elevitch and Love 2011)

Surinam cherry is a juicy, sweet-tart fruit generally considered "kid's food" for picking and eating out of hand. In Hawai'i tasting trials of unusual fruits in the early 2000s, chefs were attracted to the strong, resinous flavors of Surinam cherry and began developing unusual dishes highlighting it. By developing a market among chefs over a few years, Surinam cherry prices have increased from $1.25/lb to $6.50/lb.

Products and markets

Surinam cherry fruits are usually eaten out of hand, but are also often processed into jam, jelly, and relish. The fruit can also be pickled and the juice is fermented in wine or vinegar. Some chefs use the fruit as a base for an exotic curry. Whole fruit or pieces can be used in pie, pudding, salad, and ice cream. The leaves contain a pungent oil that repels insects. Infused or decocted leaves have several medicinal uses.

Due to the quick degradation of the fruit at ambient temperatures, the faster it can move from field to refrigeration, the longer its shelf life. Fresh fruit packaged for the consumer should be in vented clamshell containers with no more than a double layer of fruit. Packed fruit should be even colored and inspected carefully for defects and possible infestation. Fruit that leaks juice should be discarded or kept for processing. Fruit harvested for sale to processors should be washed. Freshly picked Surinam cherry chilled within an hour of harvest can maintain its integrity in the produce section of a supermarket for up to 14 days.

Surinam cherry sold as fresh fruit is generally harvested when fully ripe as the fruit contains more sugar and less resin. The fruit is edible, somewhat firmer and less susceptible to damage, when the color is orange or orange-red, but has a more resinous flavor. Fruit harvested for processing can be picked as soon as it becomes orange. Chefs and jelly manufacturing companies have expressed a desire for fruit at this stage.

Multiple cropping systems

The tree can produce fruit well even in partial shade, and due to its small stature, it makes a good understory tree. Surinam cherry is also planted in hedges, which, when regularly pruned, can become dense and serve as living fences or boundary barriers in edible landscaping.

Description

Surinam cherry is a large shrub that can achieve heights in excess of 8 m (25 ft), although due to its slow growth it can take decades to reach this height. As a member of the Myrtaceae family, the plant is related to guava, jaboticaba, mountain apple and

Demand by chefs for Surinam cherry has increased over the past few years due to tasting trials conducted in 2003.

many other edible species. There are two distinct variations found in Surinam cherry, a common red colored fruit and a less resinous dark purple to black, often sweeter fruit. The tree produces fruit in full sun or partial shade.

Environment

Surinam cherry is a tropical that can be grown in tropical or subtropical regions. It can be grown at sea level up to 1,500 m (5,000 ft) in elevation. The plant has a long taproot and can survive periods of drought. The plant thrives in most soils but produces more fruit in deep loamy soil. It is intolerant of saline conditions.

Yam

Traditional starch crop

(adapted from Elevitch and Love 2011)

Yam is one of the most important staple crops of the Pacific and ranks among the top root crops in the tropics along with taros (*Colocasia* and *Xanthosoma* species) and cassava (*Manihot esculenta*). It should not be confused with sweetpotato, which is often referred to as "yam," but is a completely different species. Yam has high potential for Pacific Islander markets as well as certain niche markets, such as Japanese cuisine, where certain varieties are highly valued.

Products and markets

Yams (*Dioscorea* spp.) are largely seasonal crops primarily cultivated for their edible tubers, which are consumed as a staple food. Most species and cultivars must be cooked by boiling, frying, or roasting prior to consumption to denature toxic alkaloids. In addition to consumption as a starchy carbohydrate in dishes, yam can also be processed into flakes or flour for storage and use in food preparation. Purple-fleshed varieties are used in ice cream and confectioneries. Yam tuber also makes suitable poultry and livestock feeds. Parts of the plant are used in various folk remedies.

Avoiding mechanical damage when harvesting, handling, and transporting is important, as yam is susceptible to bruising, which limits longevity of tubers in storage and reduces the value of fresh product in the marketplace.

Local farmers markets, retail stores, and restaurants are the primary markets. Markets may be developed for yam starch, flour, or flakes to be used in special diets. For example, starch grains of *D. esculenta* are particularly small, making them more easily digestible by people with digestive disorders.

Multiple cropping systems

Yams are very commonly interplanted with other staple food plants, supplementary food crops and a range of food trees and other multipurpose trees, many of which are pollarded or coppiced, but not killed to allow for regeneration. Yams, which require high quality soils, are normally the first crop in the succession of a shifting agricultural garden, which after harvesting are succeeded by taro, sweetpotato, or cassava before a plot of land is allowed to revert to fallow. In the Pacific, yam is often planted in large intercropped communal gardens to be followed by other crops. The most common crop combinations a number of yam cultivars interplanted with taro (*Colocasia esculenta*), giant taro (*Alocasia macrorrhiza*) and the Pacific plantain (*hopa*, *Musa* AAB group). The entire garden is normally planted within and existing coconut plantation with other scattered useful trees. Sweet yam, hibiscus spinach (*Abelmoschus manihot*) and pandanus are often planted along the borders.

Yam is a traditional food of the Pacific and has potential for Pacific islander markets in Hawai'i, as well as certain varieties for Japanese and other cuisines.

Because yams require good soils and due to anthracnose wilt, the rose beetle and other diseases, yams, are normally the first in the planting sequence and only occasionally planted two or more years in succession on the same plot of land.

Description

Yams are perennial vines that are usually grown as annuals for their edible tubers and bulbils. The characteristically spiraling, winged or ridged stems, which can grow to 2–12 m long, typically twine and climb on other vegetation during the growing season. The strongly veined leaves are usually heart shaped. Tubers vary widely in size depending on species and variety. *D. alata* tubers range from cylindrical and up to 1.5 m in length, to stout, fingered or lobed. The flesh is white, cream, or purple.

Environment

Yam grows in tropical to warm temperate, frost-free climates. It prefers well-distributed rainfall of 1,500 mm. Although drought tolerant, even soil moisture is required for good tuber production. Optimum average temperatures during the growing season are 25–30°C (77–86°F). Yam does not tolerate water-logged soils and thrives best in well-drained, fertile soil rich in organic matter.

Craig Elevitch and Ken Love

RESOURCES

Hawai'i Small Business Development Centers (HSBDC)

Present on all islands and offer free business consulting services, including business consulting, research, and technical training. Expert consultants on all islands work closely with business owners to achieve successful outcomes. East Hawai'i Island, Hilo: 808-933-0776; West Hawai'i Island, Kailua-Kona: 808-327-3680; Kihei, Maui: 808-875-5990; Honolulu: 808-945-1430; Lihue, Kaua'i: 808-241-3148; Main Office, Hilo: 808-974-7515. Register at www.hisbdc.org

Agribusiness Incubator Program (AIP), University of Hawai'i

Works specifically with agricultural businesses on analysis of financial and operational performance, processes and procedures and assisting with the development of strategic and business plans. Initial consultation, strategic planning, and general business advice are provided at no cost to accepted applicants. For other services, the program charges subsidized fees. Address: 3050 Maile Way, Gilmore 115, Honolulu, Hawaii 96822; Tel: 808-956-3530; Fax: 808-956-3547; agincubator@ctahr.hawaii.edu; http://aip.hawaii.edu

Business Action Center (BAC) of Hawai'i Department of Commerce & Consumer Affairs

Can help with registering a business, trade name, trademark, or submit other filings, obtain tax licenses, register as an employer with the Department of Labor and Industrial Relations, and locate information on licenses, permits, and registration requirements for state, county, and federal governments. Also provides information about business counseling and workshops offered by other agencies and resources available to business owners. Has offices on in Honolulu, Kahului, and Hilo. www.hawaii.gov/dcca/bac

Small Business Innovation Research Program (SBIR)

A highly competitive program that encourages small business to explore their technological potential and provides the incentive to profit from its commercialization. INNOVATE Hawaii guides Hawai'i businesses through the proposal process via trainings and connections with qualified consultants, prevetted through their Business Consultant Program. www.htdc.org/sbir/

Pacific Business Center Program (PBCP), University of Hawai'i

Provides a wide range of management and technical assistance to clients from Hawai'i and throughout the Pacific Islands who are starting up, revitalizing or expanding small and large businesses. Services include business planning and feasibility studies, market research and strategies, and financial planning. A number of *pro bono* consultations are available to small Hawai'i enterprises each year. Tel: 808-956-6286; Email: pbcp@hawaii.edu; www.pbcphawaii.com

SCORE

A nonprofit association comprised of 13,000+ volunteer business counselors throughout the U.S. and its territories. SCORE members are trained to serve as counselors, advisors, and mentors to aspiring entrepreneurs and business owners. Services are provided free of charge. www.sba.gov/content/score

Hawai'i Department of Health, Food and Drug Branch

An inspection and regulatory agency for food establishments including commercial processing kitchens. Permit applications and guidelines are available on the web site. Generally not set up to advise and assist farmers. Some offices can help with labeling requirements, and may be willing to give feedback on a proposed label. O'ahu: 808-586-4725; Hawai'i Island: 808-933-0917; Maui: 808-984-8233; Kaua'i: 808-241-3323; Moloka'i, Lāna'i: 808-553-3208. www.hawaii.gov/health/environmental/sanitation/

U.S. Food and Drug Administration Food Labeling and Nutrition Overview

Covers labeling regulations for prepared and processed foods including requirements and exemptions: www.fda.gov/Food/LabelingNutrition/default. htm Dietary supplements are covered separately here: www.fda.gov/Food/DietarySupplements/default. htm

USDA Food Safety and Inspection Service Labeling Guidelines

Provides guidance primarily pertaining to labeling of meat, poultry, and egg products:

www.fsis.usda.gov/regulations/Labeling_Guidance/index.asp

USDA Organic Certification portal

Provides certification information for producers, handlers, processors, retailers, and consumers: www.usda.gov/wps/portal/usda/usdahome?navid=ORGANIC_CERTIFICATIO

Agricultural Marketing Resource Center (AgMRC)

Provides science-based and unbiased marketing information to U.S. ranchers and farmers, including the topic of food packaging strategies, innovative food packaging solutions and resources for commercial kitchens and small co-packers. Agricultural Marketing Resource Center 1111 NSRIC, Iowa State University, Ames, IA 50011-3310. Tel: 866-277-5567; Email: AgMRC@iastate.edu agmrc.org; www.agmrc.org

REFERENCES

Arruda, K. 2011. Food Labeling. Presentation given at "Successful Branding, Marketing, and More of Value-Added Products," April 26, 2011, Kona–NELHA Conference Room, Kailua-Kona, Hawai'i.

Bittenbender, H.C., and E. Kling. 2009. Making Chocolate from Scratch. Publication FST-33. College of Tropical Agriculture and Human Resources (CTAHR), UH Mānoa, Honolulu.

Boland, M. 2009. What is value-added agriculture? Kansas State University, Kansas. www.agmrc.org/ business_development/getting_prepared/valueadded_agriculture/articles/index.cfm

Born, H. and J. Bachmann. 2006. Adding Value to Farm Products: An Overview. National Center for Appropriate Technology (NCAT), Butte, MT. www.attra.ncat.org/attra-pub/valueovr.html

Chan-Halbrendt, C., J. Krishnakumar, Q.A. Zhang, and Ken Love. 2010. Advancing Sales of Hawai'i-Grown Avocados Through Labeling. Publication F_N-16. College of Tropical Agriculture and Human Resources (CTAHR), UH Mānoa, Honolulu.

Cox, Linda J. 1996. "Your Cost of Production and Product Pricing." This Hawaii Product Went to Market. eds. James R. Hollyer, Jennifer L. Sullivan, and Linda J. Cox. College of Tropical Agriculture and Human Resources, pp. 36-39.

Elevitch, C.R., and H.I. Manner. 2006. Artocarpus heterophyllus (jackfruit), ver. 1. In: Elevitch, C.R. (ed.). Species Profiles for Pacific Island Agroforestry. Permanent Agriculture Resources (PAR), Hōlualoa, Hawai'i. www.traditionaltree.org

Elevitch, C.R. (ed.). 2011. Specialty Crops for Pacific Islands. Permanent Agriculture Resources, Holualoa, Hawai'i. www.agroforestry.net/scps

Elevitch, C.R., and K. Love. 2011. Farm and Forestry Production and Marketing Profiles: Highlighting value-added strategies. Permanent Agriculture Resources (PAR), Holualoa, Hawai'i.

Elevitch, C., N. Milne, and J. Cain. 2012. Hawai'i Island Farmer's Guide to Accessing Local Markets. Hawai'i Community College Office of Continuing Education and Training, Center for Agricultural Success, and Permanent Agriculture Resources. www.hawaiihomegrown.net/pdfs/Hawaii-Island-Guide-to-Accessing-Markets.pdf

Enay, S. 2011. "Finding Your Way into the Food Business: 6 steps to getting your food product to market." Hawaii Business Magazine. www.hawaiibusiness.com/SmallBiz/December-2011/Finding-Your-Way-into-the-Food-Business/index.php

Ernst, M. and T. Woods. 2011. Adding Value to Plant Production—An Overview. University of Kentucky Department of Agricultural Economics, Lexington, KY. www.ca.uky.edu/agecon/index.php

Federal Trade Commission. 2001. Selling 'American-Made' Products? What Businesses Need to Know

About Making Made in USA Claims. Bureau of Consumer Protection, Office of Consumer and Business Education. http://business.ftc.gov/sites/default/files/pdf/alt101-selling-american-made-products-made-usa-claims.pdf

Fleming, K. 2002. Coffee cost of production spreadsheet. www.ctahr.hawaii.edu/oc/freepubs/spreads/coffee$.xls

Fleming, K. 2005. Value-Added Strategies: Taking Agricultural Products to the Next Level AB-16. College of Tropical Agriculture and Human Resources (CTAHR), UH Mānoa, Honolulu.

Fleming, K., V. Easton Smith, and H.C. Bittenbender. 2009. The Economics of Cacao Production in Kona. University of Hawai'i Department of Tropical Plant and Soil Sciences, Honolulu. www.ctahr.hawaii.edu/oc/freepubs/pdf/AB-17.pdf

Gold, M. and R.S. Thompson. 2011. Alternative Crops & Enterprises for Small Farm Diversification. USDA Alternative Farming Systems Information Center, Beltsville, MD. www.nal.usda.gov/afsic/pubs/altlist.shtml

Gross, K.C., C.Y. Wang, and M. Saltveit. 2004 (revised). The Commercial Storage of Fruits, Vegetables, and Florist and Nursery Stocks. Agriculture Handbook Number 66. USDA-ARS, Beltsville, MD. www.ba.ars.usda.gov/hb66/

Hollyer, J.R., J.L. Sullivan, and L.J. Cox. 1996. This Hawaii Product Went to Market. UH College of Tropical Agriculture and Human Resources, Honolulu.

Kitinoja, Lisa and Adel A. Kader. 2003. Small-Scale Postharvest Handling Practices: A Manual for Horticultural Crops (4th Edition). University of California, Davis.

Kobayashi, K. and H.C. Bittenbender. No date. Farmer's Bookshelf: Information on Tropical Crop Production in Hawaii. Department of Tropical Plant and Soil Sciences, University of Hawai'i, Honolulu. www.ctahr.hawaii.edu/fb/fb.html

Love, K. no date. Harvest Avocados at the Right time! www.hawaiifruit.net/HarvestattheRighttime.htm

Love, K. 2003. Protective Fruit Wrapping. Love Family Farms, Kona, Hawaii. www.hawaiifruit.net/bag_report.htm

Love, K., R. Bowen, and K. Fleming. 2007. Twelve Fruits with Potential Value-Added and Culinary Uses. College of Tropical Agriculture and Human Resources (CTAHR), UH Mānoa, Honolulu. www.ctahr.hawaii.edu/oc/freepubs/pdf/12fruits.pdf

Love, K. and R.E. Paull. 2011a. Bilimbi. Publication F_N-23. College of Tropical Agriculture and Human Resources (CTAHR), UH Mānoa, Honolulu. www.ctahr.hawaii.edu/Site/Info.aspx

Love, K. and R.E. Paull. 2011b. Jackfruit. Publication F_N-19. College of Tropical Agriculture and Human Resources (CTAHR), UH Mānoa, Honolulu. www.ctahr.hawaii.edu/Site/Info.aspx

Love, K. and R.E. Paull. 2011c. Rollinia. Publication F_N-21. College of Tropical Agriculture and Human Resources (CTAHR), UH Mānoa, Honolulu. www.ctahr.hawaii.edu/Site/Info.aspx

Love, K. and R.E. Paull. 2012. How to price your crops for a fair profit based on cost of production. College of Tropical Agriculture and Human Resources (CTAHR), UH Mānoa, Honolulu. www.ctahr.hawaii.edu/oc/freepubs/pdf/ET-13.pdf

Martin, F.W. no date. Selecting the right crop for your location in the tropics or in the subtropics. ECHO, Florida. www.echocommunity.org/resource/resmgr/a_to_z/azch1sel.htm

Melrose, J. and D. Delparte. 2012. Hawai'i County Food Self-Sufficiency Baseline 2012. University of Hawai'i at Hilo, Geography and Environmental Studies Department. http://geodata.sdal.hilo.hawaii.edu/GEODATA/COH_Ag_Project.html

Peterson, A.R., K.R. Sharma, S.T. Nakamoto, and P. Leung. 1999. Production Costs of Selected Vegetable Crops in Hawaii (Cabbage, Cucumber, Green Onion, and Lettuce). AB-13. Department of Food Science and Human Nutrition, UH Mānoa. www.ctahr.hawaii.edu/hnfas/publications/agribusiness/productionCostsVeg.pdf

Purdue University. 2011. NewCROP. www.hort.purdue.edu/newcrop

Ragone, D. 2011. Farm and Forestry Production and Marketing Profile for Breadfruit (*Artocarpus altilis*). In: Elevitch, C.R. (ed.). Specialty Crops for Pacific Island Agroforestry. Permanent Agriculture Resources (PAR), Holualoa, Hawai'i. www.agroforestry.net/scps

Sato, D., N. Ikeda, and T. Kinoshita. 2007. Home-Processing Black and Green Tea (*Camellia sinensis*).

Document FST-326. College of Tropical Agriculture and Human Resources (CTAHR), University of Hawai'i at Mānoa, Honolulu.

Smith, V.E., S. Steiman, and C.R. Elevitch. 2009. Farm and Forestry Production and Marketing Profile for Coffee (*Coffea arabica*). In: Elevitch, C.R. (ed.). Specialty Crops for Pacific Islands. Permanent Agriculture Resources (PAR), Holualoa, Hawai'i. www.agroforestry.net/scps

State of Hawai'i Department of Health. 2009 (revised). Basic Guidelines for Food Labeling. Food and Drug Branch, Honolulu.

UH CTAHR. Publication and Information Central, search for "cost of production." www.ctahr.hawaii.edu/Site/Info.aspx

USDA Economic Research Service. 2011. Food Dollar Series. www.ers.usda.gov/data-products/food-dollar-series/food-dollar-application.aspx

USDA Economic Research Service. 2012. Organic Market Overview. www.ers.usda.gov/topics/natural-resources-environment/organic-agriculture/organic-market-overview.aspx

USDA NASS. 2010. Statistics of Hawaii Agriculture 2008. Hawaii Field Office, Honolulu. www.nass.usda.gov/Statistics_by_State/Hawaii/index.asp

AUTHORS

Craig Elevitch has been an educator in agroforestry since 1991. He was the grain miller and business director at a certified Biodynamic® farm in southern Sweden 1984–88, where he gained his first experiences producing and marketing value-added products. From 1993 to 2003 he operated AgroForester™ Tropical Seeds, which produced and sold Hawai'i-grown tree seed to farmers and organizations in over 80 countries. He currently directs Agroforestry Net, a nonprofit educational organization dedicated to empowering people in agroforestry and ecological resource management. The organization's internationally recognized publications and workshops have guided thousands in becoming more proficient in ecological food production, agroforestry, and enterprise development. His books include *Agroforestry Guides for Pacific Islands* (2000), *The Overstory Book: Cultivating Connections with Trees* (2004), *Traditional Trees of Pacific Islands: Their Culture, Environment, and Use* (2006), and *Specialty Crops for Pacific Islands* (2011), all of which document diverse agricultural systems that produce abundant food, fiber, medicine for subsistence and commercial purposes.

Ken Love, widely known as a passionate tropical fruit expert, is co-owner of Love Family Farms in Kona, Hawai'i, which produces a range of value-added products including jams, jellies, dried fruits, and coffee. As an educator, he works to promote crop diversification programs. His research supports farmers in becoming sustainable though diversity, agritourism and value-added product development. Ken has held presentations on these programs in the South Pacific, Japan, India and Italy. He is Executive Director of Hawaii Tropical Fruit Growers, which has almost 700 members statewide. He is also President of the American Culinary Federation Kona Kohala Chefs Association and chairs the Agriculture Committee. Ken's publications include a popular series of fruit variety posters for avocado, citrus, fig, and banana. He was also developer and project coordinator for the 12 Trees Project, which promotes underutilized tropical fruits for high-end markets. Out of the project, he developed a series of chef guides and he has been known to don a chef's uniform and toque when called upon to do so. Ken co-stars in *The Fruit Hunters*, a 2012 documentary film that highlights well known tropical fruit fanatics worldwide.